The
MYTH
of the
SHIKSA
AND
OTHER ESSAYS

The
MYTH
of the
SHIKSA
AND
OTHER ESSAYS

EDWIN H. FRIEDMAN

To:
The Rev. Denine Schiavone
Congratulation on your ordination
as a deacon in Christ's One,
Holy, Catholic and Apostolic
Church.

From:

Church Publishing
NEW YORK

Church Publishing
19 East 34th Street
New York, NY 10016
www.churchpublishing.org

Library of Congress Cataloging-in-Publication Data

Friedman, Edwin H.
    The myth of the Shiksa and other essays / Edwin H. Friedman.
        p.   cm.
    Includes bibliographical references.
    ISBN 978-1-59627-077-0 (pbk.)
    1. Family–Religious life. 2. Family psychotherapy. I. Title.
BL625.6.F76 2008
158–dc22

                                                    2007039246

Printed in the United States of America

CONTENTS

GROWING UP FRIEDMAN

A Foreword by Shira Friedman Bogart

Nobody ever liked my father. He had such a polarizing effect that people either adored and revered him or were appalled by his often maverick theories. But he was as irreverent about ideological popularity as he was about his trademark fashion sense — white socks with an ill-fitting suit. "How can I make an impact on society unless I turn it on its *tuchous?*" he would implore. It was all a puzzle. Each idea led to another and my father was just piecing it all together. He insisted there were no new ideas, just new pairings of them.

This made him a landmine of paradox: a minister's rabbi, a therapist's ego, an enemy's friend. If you meandered unsuspectingly through his thought process, something would surely detonate. He would drop ideas into conversation, ideas he was often just trying out to see what they'd ignite.

I once found a collection of written evaluations of some of his lectures. They began as complimentary: *a visionary, great use of the human condition, my favorite seminar.* As I poured through these responses, I was bathed in naive pride. And then, without warning, the father I knew reared his shiny head — *I found the presenter arrogant, confusing, politically incorrect.* Ah yes, this was the father I remember! This was the father I spent my childhood and young adulthood trying to impress, the man for whom I selected a career in writing and traveled the world to prove my sense of adventure. Bold, irreverent, unafraid. He brushed with fate, did not adhere to rules he did not personally create, and loved to provoke — thoughts, anger, joy, just thinking differently. The man who could write "How to Succeed in Therapy without Really Trying," interview Satan as "The First Family Counselor," and dare to challenge Jewish lore with "The Myth of the Shiksa."

I used to think my family was typical. Didn't everyone discuss the dysfunctional relationship between a football coach and his wide receivers at the dinner table? And what is so surprising about a rabbi who zips his sports car into his allotted parking spot at Temple with a handful of speeding tickets and skid marks in his wake? It was as if we had our own Commandments with the "original sin" as the seduction of self. Our edicts included directives like: *Thou shalt not blame others for your own insecurities / Thou shalt learn and grow from challenge / Thou shalt not will change.* And the ever popular, *Thou shalt make an impact on society.*

I had my first encounter with Dad's thought process while preparing for my Bat Mitzvah. Left alone to write my speech, I thought the *Encyclopaedia Britannica* could say it much better than I. My father might have ignored this brush with plagiarism, but it was my perspective on God that got him spinning. He sent me back to my desk, armed with a pencil and a heady conversation, to write my unique views. Today, I can trace my ability to take "facts" and bend them into new forms to that thorny encounter with my father, who taught me to be more concerned with critical thinking than with data.

Retrospectively, it now seems obvious that my father was grooming me to be a writer. Not only did our family mix metaphors, we also played an endless round of the "synonym and homonym game." I don't exactly remember what the prize was, but I was so conditioned that whenever I came upon words that sounded the same, I would burst out of my room chanting my discoveries out loud. A well-injected curse word was also quite acceptable when it came to verbal expression. I seem to recall that "bitch" was the highest compliment my father could pay me — it meant that my progression of thought had mixed with sentence structure to render him speechless. Ultimately, it meant I had one-upped him. A lifetime goal, I suppose.

But responsibility trumped words. As so many of his writings show, from "Empathy Defeats Therapy" to *A Failure of Nerve,* my father was resolute in his assertion that words are empty without the motivation to elicit change. Still, one can imagine what it was like trying to sneak a sweet but superficial liaison into the family only to be met with responses like, "Sure, go ahead and marry him. But you'll spend the rest of your life trying to define yourself to such a no-self!"

Early on my father worried that perfect little Shira, so concerned with following the rules, would turn out lawless as an adolescent and young adult. So at the age of five, when I decided that the living room drapes would be far more efficient for someone of my height with a small hole cut in the center, my mother hollered at the discovery, but my father dripped relief. In his mind, through that small hole in the curtains an encouraging future came pouring in. A future packed with missteps and exploration.

But then came adolescence and a gravitational pull to fit in. With his natural penchant for individuality, my father could not understand why I was suddenly altering my very core to blend in with the other teenage lemmings. Although I knew he was right, a date for the prom was far more crucial than my personal growth. Undeterred, he was constantly at me to define myself. At first I learned to just "talk the talk" to get him off my back, as I told my fellow lemmings — until years later I realized I was living the talk as well. I had created my own being.

As college loomed, it came to my father's attention that he didn't know many of my girlfriends. Since I had few secrets from him, I openly explained that our evenings usually revolved around André pink champagne and a drinking game of "Quarters." As he wrote in essays like "Secrets and Systems," my father was adamant that the truth hurts less than the anxiety of not knowing. So he processed this information for about a day and then offered up our home as the new site of our gatherings — provided cabs were called when everyone had to leave. Although secretly fearful that our alcoholic consumption seemed a bit gluttonous, he never let on but maintained that nonanxious presence that became his trademark phrase.

It was not the first time I had met with real-life application of his theories. Years earlier I experienced his use of paradox, or what he learned as "reversal" from his mentor, Murray Bowen (see "Mischief, Mystery, and Paradox"). In an effort to get more attention at home, I tried my hand at shoplifting. Although I was successful in getting caught, my father saw through my ruse and, when he came to spring me from the store, insisted I go see a lawyer friend of his. For a moment I had visions of juvenile detention, until he announced, "Shira, I want you to go see Paul. He can introduce you to some real hardened criminals, so you can learn how to steal without getting caught." Needless to say, my father's well-timed injection of paradox and reversal gave my new hobby less appeal.

Essays like "The Birthday Party" illustrate that my father also practiced family of origin work at home. Cousins would often emerge out of nowhere, packing stories of other random relatives that I would later meet. Perhaps because my father was an only child, a second cousin once removed had as much clout as a niece. It was about relationships and a continuing connection from generation to generation.

I didn't know how important I was to my father until I first introduced him to my husband. Back in the days when you could actually greet people as they hobbled off the plane, my father emerged wearing a trench coat, a tennis sweater, his beloved New Balance running shoes, and his famous comb-over. My husband-to-be stood immobilized, trying to ascertain whether he was in the presence of Einstein or the Jewish Mafia. When I later told my father that my boyfriend had been nervous about the meeting, he replied, "Me too!" But there was more. My mother later told me that he returned to Maryland, proclaimed that he had just met his future son-in-law, and commenced to cry. After many boyfriends, thousands of miles, and twenty-seven years, no theory could fix the feeling that he was losing his little girl.

When my father died suddenly in 1996 of a heart attack, I had no regrets and no issues to resolve — just a huge, painful void that showed up in my mitral valve as a heart murmur. Of course, if my father had known of this physiological outcome he would have said to me, "Oh, Shira. You have got to differentiate yourself. I'm just too important to you." But in truth, I think he would have been delighted how much I miss him.

ACKNOWLEDGMENTS

It is a great pleasure for me that this collection of essays has been made available by Church Publishing. My father considered these his "Best of Ed" compilation and would have been delighted to see them all together in bound form.

Many thanks go to Ryan Masteller, Managing Editor, for turning the original antiquated copies into usable form and for creating a thoroughly seamless production process. In addition, I would like to thank Cynthia Shattuck for her editorial prowess and for her unique ability to leverage my father's tone.

I would also like to express my gratitude to Myrna Carpenter at The Center for Family Process for asking me to speak at the 2006 conference honoring the ten-year passing of my father. It is on that speech, "Growing Up Friedman," that the introduction to this book is based.

I must also thank my mother for ensuring that these essays were kept alive. And thanks to my father, whose vision, passion, and unrelenting need to express his ideas made this book possible.

Shira Friedman Bogart

The
MYTH
of the
SHIKSA
AND
OTHER ESSAYS

One

AN INTERVIEW WITH
THE FIRST FAMILY COUNSELOR

Having been involved in marriage and family therapy for almost thirty years, I thought it appropriate that I give a historical perspective by seeking out and interviewing the first creature in history to give advice to a married couple. Since all rabbis are given three outrageous wishes after ordination, and I had used up only one, I decided to cash in my second and received permission for this interview. I can't tell you where it took place, but I can say it was over a period of several months.

First, an etymological note. In Hebrew the word "Satan" is pronounced *sah-tahn*. It is not a name but the noun form of a verb that means "to entice," or to be an "adversary." The grammatical form *sah-tahn* means, literally, one whose profession is to tempt, entice, or be adversarial. In rabbinic literature the term *sitra achra* is often used instead, lest by calling Satan by name one might invoke him. *Sitra achra* means "the other side." It has always intrigued me that the late Dr. Murray Bowen's understanding of paradox was an effort to get on "the other side" of the madness you are confronting, which he called a "reversal."

I

FRIEDMAN: *Satan, let me begin by thanking you for your willingness to grant this interview.*

SATAN: It's my pleasure, just as long as you don't make fun of me. I can't stand it when people don't take me seriously.

Originally conceived for the keynote address at the "Dialogue 94" National Conference of Pastoral Counselors, Milwaukee, Wisconsin, May 1994.

You mean like C. S. Lewis or George Bernard Shaw?

On the contrary; they captured my spirit completely, unlike that Job fellow. You know, he still doesn't accept the fact that I exist.

Why should that bother you?

You're right. I used to think I could throw people off course only if they believed in me; now I find it works better if they deny my existence completely.

I'd like to start with a rather simple question. I've always wondered why you began with Eve. Why didn't you go straight to Adam and give him the fruit yourself?

That is not such a simple question. I really didn't expect her to give it to him. That's precisely what I was afraid she would do.

You were using paradox?

Yes, but I was new at it. I had yet to refine my technique. The outcome was the exact opposite of what I expected; why would I have wanted them to know the difference between good and evil?

Go on.

I could see right from "the beginning" — the second version is correct, by the way — they were created simultaneously — that the male of this species was not going to be the more aggressive one. Frankly, Adam was passive as hell. He would have stayed in that Garden till the end of time. Eve, on the other hand, had fire in her, desire, a sense of adventure, curiosity. And I realized if I was going to have to choose between an eternal struggle with this new species or absolute boredom forever, I'd better choose the former. Besides, the Creator wanted it that way.

He was using you?

If you must know, unlike some of the other gods, such as Mars or Venus or Neptune, this One makes life very difficult for himself. He wants his creatures to grow.

Then there are other gods?

Not in this universe. They all originally trained here and then went on to create their own worlds. Like Elohim they created their creatures in their own image. The difference was in the problem of reproduction. In Venus's world everyone loves all the time; in Mars's world they are perpetually at war. But Elohim wanted to try something different. The Creator saw himself as a God of individuation, of differentiation, of process; life was always to be in the act of becoming; the creatures might even be seen as co-creators. The problem was you can't clone differentiation no matter how well differentiated the primary copy. Every parent knows that. So the critical component in the plan was that life was always to be challenging, and the secret to the process of becoming was in a creature's response to challenge.

Then you were really working for the Creator. That must have been before the Fall.

Actually, I slipped.

Right into the choir, I understand.

But to get back to your original question — why I gave advice to Eve rather than going directly to Adam — I knew I would never be able to stop the Creator's overall plan, but I thought I might really be able to frustrate it, if I could screw up relationships.

So you created the first marital triangle?

Exactly. Why, if I had gone directly to Adam, or had dealt with Eve one on one, they both might have started dealing with one another in very mature ways. But I saw that if somehow I could get all caught up in their relationship, I might keep them stuck forever. And I am proud to say that most counselors have followed in my footsteps ever since.

I'm not sure I'll include that comment in the final version.

Anyway, the outcome was more than I could have hoped for. Each one immediately started to blame rather than take responsibility for their own response. I couldn't believe it. All either one would have had to do was take a stand, any well-defined position on what they believed, own it, and I'd have been out of there. I'd have lost all my influence.

They were both only-children.

No. No. It was much deeper than that. I sensed immediately that it would show up everywhere, almost as though it were a natural part of their basic makeup, a flaw in creation, perhaps. Only-children have no monopoly on immaturity. But the exciting thing was I now knew the key to retarding the evolution of the entire species. Something that would work no matter what the age, the gender, the race, or the ethnic background.

You seem to be suggesting that if there were some original sin that has been transmitted down through the generations, it was not an act of disobedience, which, after all, could also be seen as an act of differentiation, but their response after they had disobeyed.

You got it.

Aren't you afraid to tell me this? I mean, if the truth got out, things might swing against you.

Are you kidding? The failure of humans to take responsibility for their own emotional being and destiny is so much a part of their heritage that I can't imagine how their simply knowing it would change things.

But that's precisely what most counselors are engaged in doing. Trying to make people aware, giving them advice, pointing out their mistakes.

My best ploys.

Wait a minute, are you saying that you try to retard the evolution of the human species by tempting the helping professions into trying to help?

I do have to admit that sometimes when I am absolutely drenched in the self-sacrifice all around me, I get to thinking maybe the Holy One put troubled people on earth in order to give the good people something to do, but it's a bit more complicated than that. Actually, I have a whole series of maneuvers, and I have to be resilient enough to adapt to the age, but, basically, I always work in the same direction.

What's that?

To prevent people from reaching the essential position that is at the beginning of any mature religious philosophy.

Namely?

I will not make my salvation dependent on the functioning of others. And that works two ways. It means not *using* other people as the way to one's own salvation, and it means not *saving* other people as the way to one's own salvation.

That almost sounds like a philosophy of parenting.

Of course; they're congruent. That's why I keep parents all focused on the child instead of on themselves, getting caught up in issues like what's the right method, who's got the best statistical data, what's the right proportion of leniency and strictness?

Sounds like counselors.

As I said, they're congruent. . . . In all events, by keeping parents — and counselors — focused on the child, particularly on symptoms, I help them avoid the essential position at the beginning of a mature philosophy of parenting.

. . . and that is?

That the children who are doing best in this world — and by best I don't necessarily mean the highest grades or the most awards but rather those who are working through the natural struggles of growing and being with the least amount of reactivity towards others — the children who are doing best in this world are those whose parents made them least important to their own salvation.

That sure is an interesting parallel between theology and therapy.

And let me add that the Creator himself struggled for centuries before he was able to work that one through. But, as I said, that's what distinguishes the Holy One from all the other gods.

I'd like to hear how you go about diverting the human species from seeing what's important.

As long as you give me my due.

Guaranteed, but before we leave the Garden I do have one trivial point of curiosity.

Yes?

I've always wondered what kind of fruit was really on that tree. I mean, ever since that damn painting everyone assumes it was an apple, but the text only says fruit. Was it a pear, an orange, a tangerine, a grape, a pomegranate, or was it really an apple?

It was an avocado.

An avocado? Why on earth — pardon the expression — an avocado?

I wanted them to have a yen for things that were fattening.

Your irreverence is outrageous.

Remaining authentic is very important to me.

Let's get back to your methods. Just how do you ply your trade?

First, you must remember that I rarely do things head-on. Direct confrontation is not my bag. I saw immediately that this species with its immense intelligence and capacity for knowledge could never be led astray simply by ideas. Therefore, I always work *with* their intelligence rather than *against* it. Perversity is my game. In fact, I learned rather quickly that I could use their intelligence, and their good will, I might add, against themselves.

Could you give an example?

My primary tactic is to get flesh and blood to focus on the wrong information, on data, for example, rather than maturity, or on empathy rather than responsibility, or on self as a category of narcissism rather than a matter of integrity. I was going to say that things were different centuries ago when my main area of interest was religion....

You've gone elsewhere?

Oh yes. Now I'm primarily into counseling, any kind of counseling — marriage counseling, family counseling, pastoral counseling, organizational counseling, family business counseling. The more I can get people to rely on expertise, the more it atrophies their capacity to be decisive. The rise of the consulting industry today is a direct result of my efforts to make people afraid to take a stand. I started to say that it was different back then, before I moved over into therapy, but as we speak I begin to realize it really wasn't.

What is it that hasn't changed?

I still infiltrate by seducing people into focusing on the wrong issues, and flesh and blood still responds in the same way. It absolutely cannot resist the temptation. Over the centuries, the institutions of salvation may change form (saints, holy works, sacred rites, criteria for heresy) but the problems are the same, the spectrum of approaches is the same — so insight vs. behavior replaces faith vs. works — those false dichotomies work every time. And the fact of the matter is I'm just as successful in thwarting growth now as I was then.

You were going to explain how you go about this.

To begin with, you must remember what I said before. The Creator of this universe, unlike other gods, was not content to clone his image. Being a God of process, the Holy One wanted his creatures to be constantly in the act of becoming. This necessitated a world of absolute freedom, and it meant that the key to life was the response to challenge, but — and I want to emphasize this or you won't understand the method in my madness, so to speak — the issue of response was not simply of survival but of growth. The whole point of challenge was not simply that difficulties were to be overcome, or nullified, but to be experienced in such a way that the encounter with adversity actually fostered further growth, a higher development of the soul, increased maturity, and so on.

That's the way the immunological system operates. It learns from its battles. You seem to be suggesting an internal focus rather than an external one.

Correct. Everything that's true about immunology is true about self. That's the great hidden message in creation. I'll say more about that later. For the moment just try to understand that if what the Holy One wanted in his creatures was a constantly evolving state of maturity — which, since the Garden, the Creator has viewed in terms of the capacity to take responsibility for one's own being and destiny — then it was clear to me that anything I could do to entice creatures away from that perspective would be successful in retarding the evolution of the soul.

A quick example here would help.

Well, a quick one would be making involvement in some cause an excuse for personal awareness.

I see.

But I don't want to get all bogged down in method; that's precisely what I'm always seducing others into doing. My game is much bigger than that. I have always known that one of the best ways to hinder evolution was to create societies of intimidation because that gets everyone to herd; it creates undifferentiated globbiness; it induces a big push for togetherness and community all right, but it's more a stuck-togetherness, a togetherness that nurtures the kinds of communities that inhibit self-realization.

Yet you have the reputation of being against community and behind all acts of selfishness, egotism, narcissism, and pride.

One of my best tricks. Getting humanity to create communities is precisely what I want. It's the kind of communities I want them to create that is the important issue. You see, it's really quite easy to get flesh and blood to come together; all protoplasm loves to join. The problem for humanity is not getting close, it's preserving self, by which I mean integrity, in a close relationship. That's the basic issue. For years I used to bring about undifferentiated communities by fostering totalitarian regimes; there was always an infinite supply of self-aggrandizing organisms around to inspire to become false saviors. But it got too bloody. In recent years, however, I have come to realize that that approach is very inefficient and that you don't need totalitarian governments to create monolithic societies.

What works better?

Raising society's level of anxiety and encouraging PC.

Do you mean political correctness or pastoral counseling?

Sometimes they're hard to distinguish.

But can't anxiety be challenging?

I'm not talking about that kind of anxiety — the kind that is connected with a goal. I'm talking about chronic anxiety, the kind that is nonspecific; the kind that just grips everyone like an overall atmosphere. The kind that increases automatic reactivity of everyone to everyone; the kind that increases blaming rather than owning; the kind that creates surges of quick-fix attitudes; the kind that gets everyone to herd. The kind that inhibits the expression or development of well-defined leadership. But raising society's level of anxiety only sets the scene, and here you will see the essence of my genius — the more anxious I can make society, the easier it becomes for me to tempt creatures into violating the nature of their being, and that's when I've really got them.

I'm still not getting it.

Look at it this way. If you read the accounts of creation carefully, you will see that the Creator established three principles to separate a god from a human. It doesn't matter what kind of human, black or white, Jewish or Christian, male or female. The three criteria have to do with knowledge, power, and death. Whereas gods can be omniscient, omnipotent, or immortal, human beings cannot be all-knowing, all-powerful, or live eternally. Whenever they disregard, no less try to violate, those basic parameters of existence, they lose their way.

So you're saying that almost all barriers to community result from trying to will what can't be willed.

In a way, but let me get to the overarching theme here. It is when human beings become most anxious that they are most liable to forget what makes them human, and then they're really in my power.

If I get your drift, what you are saying is that you do not want human beings to acknowledge or perhaps even face their frailty. You want them to think that as long as they have enough power or enough knowledge or enough time, they could solve anything.

Precisely. All my temptations work best when humans keep trying to solve what they cannot solve, rather than growing from the acceptance of their limitations.

Satan, sometimes you sound like a preacher.

Darth Vader was once a Jedi Knight.

II

Talk more about the dark side.

Very well. I have designed a whole set of temptations to fit those three natural limitations of the human condition: omniscience, omnipotence, and immortality, which as I said become more tempting as anxiety increases. If you want, I'll explain how I have structured each set, but let me warn you, you're going to find some of this very disturbing.

I'll just pretend you're not telling the truth.

Fair enough. To begin with: omniscience. What I do here is to get the human species to equate the mind — or more narrowly the cortex — with the soul.

As with the word "psyche"?

Ah, that one word helps immeasurably. It originally referred to the soul, but I have gotten the social sciences to equate it with the mind.

As in psychology, psychiatry, and psychosomatic?

By getting humans to think that their thought processes are the key to everything, I get them first of all to overlook the emotional processes that might be driving their thinking processes. That, in turn, furthers the absurd dichotomy between body and soul, which, as you may know, goes against all the new findings that the brain is the largest organ of secretion, sending messages to and receiving messages from all parts of the body simultaneously. Not even memory is solely in the brain. In all events I have succeeded just through that one word, "psyche," in seducing the entire eastern intellectual establishment into concentrating on all kinds of irrelevancies. I begin with the focus on IQ as a quantitative category. That one starts in grade school, determines the structure of SATs in the selection process for higher learning institutions (which also sets the selection process for who will run society), and evolves into evaluations throughout every organizational structure. From that point, it's relatively easy to get both parents and presidents to think that communication is a cerebral phenomenon depending on syntax, vocabulary, and rhetoric rather than an emotional process that depends on distance, direction, and anxiety. You know, people can't get near you unless they are moving towards you.

So that whenever you are pursuing or rescuing, your message will never catch up.

Exactly. Next I get them to focus on values rather than self-regulation. And once I've got them concentrating in this fashion, then it becomes child's play to focus them on data and method rather than on maturity and stamina. Have you any idea how many different diseases now have names? I mean emotional and physical illness. Why, I just got DSM 4, the new version of the psychiatric scriptures, to include almost a hundred new syndromes, though they left out another hundred disorders I thought up. In fifty years no one is going to be able to carry it around. But this is where the increased anxiety and the denial of human limits comes in. By overwhelming everyone with data, no one can feel adequate — and this one is also equally true for parents and presidents — so that the increased knowledge, instead of helping, adds to the anxiety. Then I work on the helping professions particularly. Focused on data rather than on their own maturity, they are easily caught up in society's quick-fix attitude and try harder and harder to "cure" everything. But of course they can't keep up. And here's the best part of all. As long as I can keep the helping professions focused on addictions such as alcohol, drugs, and abuse, rather than their own self-regulation, they can't see how their own perpetual imbibing of data and technique is the worst form of substance abuse around.

They're searching for knowledge.

Nonsense, it's not knowledge; otherwise it would lead to wisdom. Wisdom is one's accumulated response to adversity. Wisdom is not a function of information. But, you see, that's the beauty of what I've been able to tempt them into. The perseveration after data and technique keeps humans from focusing on what really would lead to wisdom. That's why it's a form of substance abuse. It makes the abuser feel better temporarily, but the very state of depending on it causes precisely those qualities that would make the substance unnecessary to atrophy.

That, sir, is absolutely devilish.

Thank you. But that's only the half of it. The real secret to my perversity is getting humans to deny theirs. The more anxious society becomes, the more they want certainty. So I delude everyone into confusing their models with reality. And I find I am equally successful everywhere. Reductionism in science and fundamentalism in religion are really the same phenomenon. The key is to make people forget that the world is essentially ambiguous, to tempt them into thinking that there are answers out there just a little beyond their reach, and that if only they tried hard, they could solve or, at least, measure anything. But the critical factors in salvation are not subject to measurement.

That one idea could put a lot of people out of work.

And there are side benefits. The more they reify their models — you know people today assume the ego and the id have substance. I've gotten them to think they're sophisticated when they give up belief in the *super*-natural, but notice how tempted they are to believe with perfect faith in the *sub*-conscious. Anyway, the more they are given to black and white, all or nothing, either/or conceptualizations of life, that really reduces the richness of their repertoire of responses, which is the key to any maturation process. And, to come full circle, once I get them thinking this way, monolithic communities form spontaneously.

Reminds me of schizophrenia.

How about idolatry? You see, I've infiltrated the social sciences as I used to infiltrate the monasteries. Instead of the social sciences being sources of direction out of the problem, I've managed to turn them into humanity's psychological defense. Just as I used to focus the clergy of yesteryear on angels-on-a-pin kind of issues, I have again succeeded in leading humanity's soul growers off track. As long as I can keep tempting everyone to fill their brains with data such as Myers-Briggs profiles, or right-brain/left-brain differences, or gender issues, or ethnic background, I can be quite sure that no one will focus on the information that counts.

And that is?

The important information categories of the soul (and they are the real bridges to community) are:

1. Knowing what you believe. I mean not only what you live for but what you'd die for.

2. Knowing where you begin and where other people who are important to you end.

3. Being able to preserve your own self, that is, having integrity, in a close relationship.

4. Having horizons that are not limited by what you can actually see.

5. Being able to stay on course when others sabotage you. By that I mean mustering up the self-regulation not to be reactive to the reactivity of others when you succeed at the above.

6. And, as I said earlier, making your own salvation dependent upon your own functioning rather than on using or saving others.

These are the information categories that count and they totally transcend social science data.

What about responsibility for others? Where does that come in?

It naturally flows from the above, because all unethical, all immoral, all manipulative behavior is really a form of dependency. The use of others means you need others to pave the path to your own salvation.

You seem to be saying that togetherness can't be willed.

Correct. That is exactly how the Creator, being a God of process, set it up, and that is why I know that the best way to frustrate his plan is to constantly seduce everybody into willing others to come together.

Like counselors?

Like counselors, like clergy, like educators, like doctors and nurses, like parents, like managers and administrators.

But what is the alternative?

Presence. The nature of one's presence — being a healing presence, a challenging presence, a nonanxious presence, the kind of presence that turns the verb "to be" into a transitive verb. Entities don't have to have moving parts in order to modify other entities.

As with catalysts, enzymes, and transformers.

Healing also is a natural phenomenon that can be promoted by the presence of the healer; it also cannot be willed. Frankly, all healing that depends on the functioning of the healer is faith-healing. But let me go on a little. These things are connected. First let me explain how I tempt flesh and blood into violating the second limitation that I was mentioning earlier, omnipotence.

I'm all ears. But before we go on, I would like to ask you something. I notice that you keep referring to the Holy One as "him." Is God then male, after all?

Don't get me started on that one.

You are opposed to liberation theology, then?

Liberation, tribulation, I couldn't care less. What bothers me is that no one has questioned *my* gender. How do you think *I* feel? Name me one solid theological work in the past twenty-five years that has suggested that I may not be patriarchal. Some of the process theologians have come close, but they've depersonalized everything. All this talk about inclusivity is just plain hypocrisy. You can't have it both ways, you know. And as long as everyone is going to keep me male, I'm not going to change my ways.

I'm sorry, I didn't realize it was going to be such a sore point. You were about to describe how you tempt human creatures into violating the boundary of omnipotence.

III

Very well. As I said, one of the major differences between a God and a human being, according to Genesis, has to do with power. A God just speaks and things come into being.

"In the beginning was the Word."

Unfortunately, it was kind of slurred. Actually, in the beginning was a thought. A God doesn't have to speak. In true omnipotence, all you have to do is think the thought, and your will becomes reality.

Sounds like the fantasy of some people I know.

Where do you think they get it from?

Transforming thought into matter is the hard part, isn't it?

You are talking about creativity. I am trying to focus on relationships. Haven't you ever noticed that the worst symptoms in families always show up in communities marked by intense will conflict? Schizophrenia, suicide, anorexia, abuse, and many physical deteriorations almost always show up in families where people are trying to will one another to change. They harp, they cajole, they seduce, they argue, they implicate, they preach, they warn, they threaten, they remind, they guilt, they charm, they accuse, they point out. Find me a polarized relationship and I will show you the will conflict.

And the same would be true for institutions?

Exactly the same. Almost all forms of neurosis and psychosis come about from the effort to will what can't be willed. You can will going to bed, but you can't will sleep. You can will going to the dinner table, but you can't will appetite. You can will physical contact, but you can't will orgasm. You can will being together, but you can't will togetherness or symptoms or relationships or morality.

So by seducing everyone into willing, you make them deny that they are not omnipotent.

Omnipotence always leads to impotence.

Why can't you apply the same to helpers?

That's what I was getting to. You can.

This is going to be good.

I no longer spend much of my time trying to get people to will one another to conform to their thoughts. I now confine myself to those who try to will them to stop willing one another. I cover far more territory that way. Instead of trying to tempt twenty different families or organizations, I just tempt their consultants. The efficiency has gone up logarithmically. You see, it is the nature of humanity to resist efforts to be willed. Nothing slows someone down faster than trying to will them to speed up. If you don't believe me, come up behind somebody in the fast lane and blow your horn hard in an effort to get them to pull over and let you by. Those "by-ways" go all the way back to the Garden.

But the kind of willing counselors do is for their own good.

Whose own good? Anyway, the intent is irrelevant. The point is, the average person will resist efforts to will them by willing the willer with equal determination to stop willing, or by applying their own will to themselves. In a way that frustrates the will of the willer.

That is utterly perverse.

If I don't say so myself.

You "snake in the grass." You have turned the good will of good people against themselves.

And I have developed a terrific support system.

I don't think I want to hear this.

I have moved up a notch to the supervisory level. The same logic that made me focus on helpers rather than clients led me to realize that if I can tempt supervisors to will their supervisees to will their clients, my efficiency would reach astronomical levels.

How do you do this?

By getting everyone to focus on method and technique, rather than the nature of their presence.

But isn't there such a thing as being a professional?

Or a hack.

And how do you distinguish between a professional and a hack?

They may both do what they do with polish. But the hack is not transformed by his experience.

I am beginning to see where you are going.

As long as I can focus helpers on the right technique, the less they are affected, themselves, by the outcome of what they do; and the more they leave out the variable of their own growth and presence, then the more they miss the Creator's focus on becoming; and the more frustrated they become at not being able to will, then the harder they try to exert their will; and the harder they try to exert their will....

I get it, I get it. The more they act like they are omnipotent. And this fits in with omniscience, doesn't it? On the one hand you get everyone to keep willing insight into unmotivated people and on the other you get publishers to perpetually produce books on technique in order to preserve the illusion of power.

Actually we have a secret agreement, the publishers and I. Recently we made a compact. They publish books full of data and technique, and I seduce everyone into violating the omnipotence limitation. It works well for both of us. It's a huge conglomerate and includes publishers in the world of therapy, religion, education, management, government.

Have you given it a name?

What would you think of Faust Publications?

Your persistence and stamina are truly extraordinary.

As with all my disciples, it comes naturally, from our lack of self-regulation. Let me give you one of my latest success stories. I have just tempted the supervision committee of the American Association for Marriage and Family Therapy to rule that all supervision must view family therapy in the context of sociological and cultural factors. In other words, the counselor and the therapist and ultimately the client must be focused on these irrelevancies to maturity.

You make it sound as though a person's background is unimportant.

Cultural camouflage is one of my greatest inventions, and the focus on cultural diversity one of my most attractive temptations. But culture is as irrelevant to maturity as gender. In fact, whenever people explain their functioning in terms of their background, that is not more information to be stored; such moments are exercises in denial of personal responsibility. As I have it now set up, many trainers with great savvy who disagree with an exclusivistic focus on culture and who might have stood in my way are going to be rejected or forced to conform their thinking to the new standards.

But that is the committee's right.

Don't you get it? I have gotten them to squelch diversity in the name of diversity. I just love the symmetry.

I suppose you would say that's one of the spin-offs of seducing people into thinking omnipotently.

Of course. It's one thing, after all, to set standards for theoretical knowledge, or clinical experience, or personal growth. That doesn't lead to omnipotence, but saying there is only one true way to do things does. Why, I haven't had such success since Torquemada, Judge Jefferies, or Cotton Mather. In religion, this would be called inquisitional, in politics it would be called totalitarian, in business monopolistic. And they're doing it in the name of heaven, or at least democracy. The AAMFT committee on supervision is going to bring back the *auto-da-fé*.

But no burning at the stake.

Today that's all done by disenfranchisement from the health insurance plans.

This may be the most disturbing thing you have said yet.

Wait till you hear what's coming.

You know, what you are saying tends to undercut the importance of gender differences. I suppose you are opposed to the women's movement.

How well I have disguised myself. On the contrary, I am delighted with all the recent freedom movements, particularly the liberation of women. Having women seek equality everywhere is just what I have been waiting for. As I said earlier, I always thought Eve had more on the ball than Adam. Equality for woman has made them more of a challenge. In the old days, women were just too easy to tempt. All I had to do was be charming. But now it's much more exciting.

Next thing I know you will tell me that feminism was your idea.

Not quite, though over the centuries I have succeeded in converting most isms into some form of idolatry, eventually.

What about Judaism?

Especially Juda*ISM*.

I fully supported the women's movement in the beginning, but then I realized that it could get out of hand. It was all right for Adam to have all of that power because he generally squandered it. But Eve and power, I saw that could really be dangerous, so I did my usual thing to throw them off course.

And you do this by . . . ?

By doing the same thing I did to the Marxists, by getting them to equate power with maturity, to confuse equality with spirituality, and to politicize intimacy.

And the temptation is?

Getting their leaders all focused on the issue of abuse.

Now wait a minute. That is absolutely ludicrous. Abuse is a very serious problem.

Obviously, men abusing women is an important issue, but it is not the most dangerous aspect of their relationship. There is something men do that is far more harmful and enslaving than physical abuse, or even the abuse of economic or political power.

That's sure news to me.

Once again, I have so well tempted flesh and blood to focus in one direction that they cannot see what is most obvious. Haven't you ever noticed that if you go into any medical building in the country, or mental health care clinic, that the women patients far outnumber the men? What do you think that's about? Only a very small percentage of those visits is driven by violence. You see, far more women have been done in by passive husbands than by violent ones. Again, it has been going on since the Garden. Women are constantly being snookered into taking the emotional responsibility for their families, for their husbands, for their children, for togetherness, for the future. Violence really has severe limits as a form of social control because ultimately it becomes intolerable, but not passivity. Especially when it is disguised by innocence and charm. That kind of stress, precisely because it is not as painful, tends to remain chronic. And chronic conditions are always far more destructive because sooner or later they become withering. . . . I see that you are speechless, so I will go on. While gaining economic power and political equality can be liberating to some extent, equality does not free people from relational binds. Ultimately the power to be free has to do with the internal factors, the inner resources I enumerated earlier.

Yes, but if your body isn't free what good is freedom of the soul?

First of all, that's reversible. Secondly, you seem to be forgetting religious history. How does it go? "Not by might, nor by power, but by my spirit."

Wow, the devil can quote scripture.

Look, my point is simply this. You asked how I tempt humanity to deny its essential nature: the fact that it is not omnipotent. And I was explaining how I seduce them into thinking in terms of power rather than soul. My success with the abuse issue is even greater than anything I did to pervert the Marxists. It has so distracted the functioning and thinking of the helping professions that I could not ask for anything more. It has produced more one-issue people than almost anything I have ever tried. The books, the conferences, the sermons, the court suits, and especially the polarization. It's wonderful! But the joke's on them. I shouldn't tell you this, but in the not too distant future men are going to become irrelevant to procreation. A major breakthrough will be made in the genetic code, and women will be able to fertilize themselves.

How could that be possible?

Even in your time there are species that reproduce parthenogenetically.

Then men won't be needed any longer. Wait till I tell some persons I know about this.

Hold on. I said they won't be needed for fertilization. Their presence will always be essential to differentiation.

You, sir, have just betrayed the fact that you are male, after all.

I didn't know ideas had gender. And you have just given the term *ad hominem* new meaning. Women, you see, have far more relational power in families then men. If only they knew how to use it. Maternal invest-ment may be the most powerful force on earth. It can promote genius or schizophrenia, talent or retardation. The male of the species is al-most invariably far more emotionally dependent. The transference from mother to wife is far more intense than that from father to husband. What women really have to do is to stop seeking confirmation from their partners and work on their differentiation from their own mothers instead. Then the power would naturally gravitate towards them.

Once again, a brief example would help.

Very well. If women want to prevent their daughters from being abused in one generation, all they have to do is stop being charmed by their sons in the previous generation.

Well, maybe we should go on to that third issue you mentioned, immor-tality. This one is a little hard for me to swallow. The way you have reframed the gender issue . . . well . . . I would have to change a lot about the way I look at life. Besides, you are coming close to treading on very sacred ground.

I suppose you mean sexual abuse in religion and therapy? Look, let me give it to you straight. Salvation has always been cunnilingual.

You are playing on the word, of course. You mean great preachers are always cunning linguists.

I know what I said. Religion, politics, therapy, they always go with sex. This is nothing new. Read Chaucer. Read *The Decameron*.

The Decameron was pre-Reformation.

And I suppose everyone stopped enjoying it after Luther. Look, go back to the Israelites. It is right there in the temple cult, temple prostitutes, male and female. He, or if you prefer, she, created them.

But they cleaned that out.

For the time. They only purified the institution. I am not talking about morality. I am just showing you how easy it is to tempt flesh and blood when they are involved in matters of the soul. Salvation has always been salacious. That's nothing new. That's why I love religion and therapy.

You know, as some traditions have it, you got pretty close to your counselee yourself.

I never touched Eve. That's one counseling tradition I will never accept responsibility for.

Then how do you explain Cain?

Bad seed. That's all. Frankly, I was more attracted to Adam. By the way, have you read the recently published correspondence between Freud and Firenze? Firenze was one of the great early theoreticians, you know. It turns out, he takes a mother and a daughter into analysis separately and winds up in bed with each of them. All institutions institutionalize the emotional processes of the founding families.

You're saying humanity can't change its institutions?

Not until they get on the other side of willing it. If you really want to stop sexual abuse in therapy and religion, open it wide up. Let everybody screw their brains out.

And I suppose you would stop speeding by getting rid of the speed limits.

And hijacking by getting rid of those damn-fool metal detectors. Force everyone to carry a gun on board.

But in every one of those cases you'd harm a lot of innocents along the way.

A small price to pay. That's a very short-sighted view. By fostering self-regulation you would nullify the power in the temptation all the way to eternity.

You want to free-float morality like the dollar. This is absurd. What's the matter with me? I've forgotten whom I'm talking to. I've allowed you to seduce me into thinking the unthinkable. Let's get on with immortality.

I can't wait.

IV

How do you pervert the third basic concept of salvation?

By introducing political rhetoric.

I have no idea what you mean.

Unlike omnipotence and omniscience, human beings *can* achieve immortality. Not as individuals, of course, but collectively, as a species. The Holy One knew that way back in the garden.

I suppose that is why he banished us.

But it was part of the process. The co-creator stuff. There are no natural limits to the growth of the soul, to maturing processes. And to the extent each generation functions in a responsible manner, the communities formed in the next generation will be that much richer for it. The process is limitless.

And by maturity, you mean what you said earlier, the capacity — or the willingness — to take responsibility for one's own emotional being and destiny.

Correct, but that means not blaming. It means understanding that the toxicity of most hostile environments is proportional to the response of the organism, not to the toxic factors within it. It also means understanding that the conditions for trauma reside within the emotional processes of the family or the community rather than within the event. It means accepting the fact that forgiving or at least not being reactive to situations is more freeing than vindication. It means understanding that cutoffs between people do more fundamental damage than the initiating hurts.

And those are all internal factors, as you said before.

Internal and eternal. They have to do with the soul, which is the proper concern of both religion and therapy.

So?

So I seduce humanity into focusing outside instead. I have three favorite displacement issues. Abuse, which I mentioned; carcinogens is the second; and the environment is the third.

Those are honest matters of concern.

I didn't say they weren't. I called them "displacement" issues, not false issues. I use them to keep people from focusing on their own salvation. I used to use the communists, but carcinogens and cholesterol work just as well. And as far as the environment goes, it is absolutely the ultimate in arrogance for humankind to think that they can destroy or save the planet. The earth will survive, even if it has to do in the human species in order to, and then it will simply start over again. If you don't believe me, pay a visit to Mount Saint Helens. The evolution of the human species does not depend on the survival of the planet; it can take care of itself. Immortality for the human species depends on overcoming its tendency to adapt to its own immaturity.

But isn't helping one's fellow, unfortunate creatures a form of maturity?

Absolutely. And there are hundreds of public and private agencies designed to accomplish that. There are *no* other institutions, however, aside from religion and therapy, that are designed for promoting the evolution of the soul. By introducing political rhetoric into salvation, I succeed in destroying their distinctiveness, and thus thwart their potential for promoting immortality. In addition, political rhetoric makes everyone get too serious, and they lose their capacity for playfulness and, therefore, perspective. Remember what I did to Marxist art? "Social realism," ughhh. Political rhetoric makes everyone more intense, it increases the efforts to will one another to change, and it enlarges the possibilities for alienation and polarization.

We're back to black and white alternatives.

Right. And most delightful for me, introducing political rhetoric into religion and therapy allows me to hoard all the devilishness for myself.

Well, I don't know what would happen to religion if it tried to get more playful. Salvation is pretty serious.

Let me correct you. What seriouses up salvation is trying to save others. Saving oneself is not nearly as grim. But I haven't finished. By introducing political rhetoric into religion and therapy, I swing the power to the dependent, to the victims, to the recalcitrant. The adaptation of the community goes towards weakness, not strength. And comfort triumphs over challenge, thus weakening the immunological response.

Why does that follow?

Because political rhetoric encourages everyone to lower their threshold for pain. It supports a quick-fix attitude. Haven't you ever noticed that in any counseling session or at any community meeting the persons most apt to mention "trust," "sensitivity," "confidentiality," "togetherness," and "consensus" are always the ones who want others to adapt to them?

These concepts have great communal potential.

They used to, but through the word "empathy" I have succeeded in turning them into abuses of power.

You're taking credit for empathy?

It's probably the most regressive concept I have ever employed.

Regressive? It's the foundation of many modern approaches to relationships.

But it makes feelings more important than boundaries. It's a very late concept, you know. The word is not even in the original edition of the *Oxford English Dictionary* published in 1931.

I believe it was originally intended as a translation of a German word in the field of aesthetics.

Came over into English about 1922, actually. At first I didn't pay too much attention to it, but then I began to realize that by getting everyone to substitute empathy for *com*passion — feeling *in* supposedly being better than feeling *with* — I saw that I could generally frustrate the Creator's plan for an evolving response to challenge because everyone would stay focused on one another instead of themselves. It wasn't until after World War II, however, that I really succeeded in getting *empathy* into common parlance.

But how does the matter of feelings connect up with immortality?

Through the concept of immunology. As some of your more recent biologists have come to realize, immunology is not basically about *outside* toxic agents; it's basically about the *inner* condition of integrity. As I said earlier, everything that is true about immunology is true about self. In fact, the immunological system has been defined as the capacity to distinguish self from nonself. It does not come equipped at birth like a woman's ovaries; it learns from its experience with adversity. Moreover, organisms that lack an immunological system cannot experience love.

Because?

Because without one it is impossible to touch another member of your own species and still retain your identity. The way the Creator set it up, when organisms of the same species that lack immunological systems even reach a certain point of proximity, one will dis-"integrate," in other words, lose its integrity, because of the presence of the other.

"Whenever you find two peas in a pod, one will begin to shrivel."

That puts it very well. But there is also an opposite form of dis-integration, the autoimmune response, which occurs when loss of self allows anxiety to flood the organism.

Hawks and doves. Pentagons can't be allowed to make the final decisions. But I still don't see where empathy comes in.

Look at it this way. What all pathogenic elements in life have in common is they lack self-regulation. This is equally true about viruses, malignant cells, substance abusers, chronically troubling members of families and institutions, and totalitarian nations. Now this characteristic is always the ground of two further attributes. One, organisms that lack self-regulation will be invasive of the space of others. Not because they want to be; it's just their nature, a byproduct of what they are missing. Two, organisms that lack self-regulation can't learn from their experience.

That fits with what you were saying earlier about trying to will insight into the unmotivated.

It's much deeper than that. Despite their essential lack of self-regulation, pathogens are really not capable of producing pathology on their own. There must also be a lack of self-regulation in the host. Remember what Churchill said about how World War II got started?

Because "the malice of the wicked was reinforced by the weakness of the virtuous."

Exactly. You see, pathogens seem to have a stamina that is hard to muster up in the virtuous. But what I realized is that it's not really stamina;

what keeps them going without let-up is lack of self-control. *And the only power that can force a mutation in the invasive organism is the exercise of self-regulation in the invaded organism.* The major nutrient of terrorism, after all, whether we are talking about families or the family of nations, is an unreasonable faith in reasonableness. What empathy has given me is a way to deceive people into avoiding responsibility for themselves, while I seem to side with the angels.

This is insidious. You're almost suggesting that the focus on empathy nourishes evil.

What do you mean "suggesting"? Look how I've gotten most Christians to interpret Jesus. His challenging statements far outnumber his comforting ones. Yet, if you go into any church in America beleaguered by pathogenic members and tell the leaders to force the irresponsible members of the community to change or leave, they respond, "empathically" it's not the Christian thing to do.

But all belief systems are open to interpretation.

It has nothing to do with Christianity. Synagogues also tolerate pathogenic elements because it's not the "Christian" thing to do. Why, I have got it to the point where people are absolutely tyrannized by the sensitivities of others. As long as I can keep everyone (especially parents) thinking about how they should *feel* for others rather than how they should prevent others from invading their "host," no one will take the kind of stands that force the unmotivated to mature.

And I suppose you would also say that such a beneficent stance is ultimately harmful to the organism one is feeling for since it deprives it of the challenging experience of transformation.

It is totally impossible for either leaders or healers to be a transforming presence in an atmosphere that values empathy over responsibility.

Then political correctness also was your idea.

Not exactly, but I immediately saw its potential for inducing a general failure of nerve. Evolution, after all, requires leaders who can stand apart from the general anxiety of the day. In fact, leaders (and parents) function as the immunological systems of their institutions. When they are well-defined, the pathogens are nowhere as quick to multiply, or, in many cases, even to form. But when leaders fail to be present, or function as an anxious presence (which is the parallel to an autoimmune response) the system cannot maintain its integrity.

You know, I think you have been talking out of both sides of your mouth. Which side are you on, anyway?

Are you accusing me of using a forked tongue?

That is a definite possibility.

Fine, don't take my word for it. But how are you going to explain all the perversity?

You want me to see people as possessed, rather than conflicted.

It's more scientific. Complexes, syndromes, disorders, they are just models. They have no substantive reality.

You mean compared to demons?

Just because an idea is learned doesn't prevent it from functioning as a superstition.

Can't you be serious for a moment?

Okay. Recently the Holy One has changed tactics and I am not sure how to handle it. For one thing, he's begun to improve the economy by having catastrophes. That's my game. I mean hurricanes, floods, tornados, massive destruction, and suddenly manna from heaven because the need for reconstruction makes job opportunities pop up everywhere. But that's not the most perverse thing he's doing. That's not what gets me most. There is something else going on, and I can't figure out how to deal with it, no how.

What's that?

Well, he's been using some damn rabbi to try to make Christians more Christian.

Wow, that is really devilish.

Devilish? It's downright satanic.

Wait till I tell people you said that!

Just remember, though, there's a theory out there that Jesus was crucified because he spoke in parables, and challenging people can make them very angry. They love answers.

All I can say is, it's an old rabbinic tradition. I'll take my chances.

Two

SECRETS AND SYSTEMS

Several years ago a newspaperman doing a piece on the CIA reported his difficulties in coming up with the most elementary information about that super-secret organization. He was unable to obtain from them even the approximate number of employees who worked there, a fact which he felt was very important to his own story. Finally, in desperation, he called the Russian Embassy and promptly got the information.

From whom, then, was the information being kept secret? Actually, as secrecy and counterespionage have become more important and more sophisticated in the relationships between governments, a rather ironic system of triangles has been established. Over and over again nations have not informed their citizenry about certain facts, for fear the enemy would find out, but the enemy has already found out, producing a situation in which the party triangled out is the citizenry. Indeed, some of this is not new at all. For as older international treaties concluded between heads of governments come to light, over and over again it turns out that there were secret provisions. In such cases again, it is the citizenry who have been triangled out and the leadership of foreign nations that have obtained a pseudo-togetherness by creating such relationship systems. Further, while it is never stated baldly, it almost appears that government leaders of different nations are in a conspiracy to help one another obtain more power over the citizens they each respectively govern. For this is how secrets work, and as I shall show, it is the ultimate purpose of secrets in families. It also provides the ultimate justification for their revelation.

I do not wish, however, to convey the impression that families act like governments. As you all know, there has been much analogizing of family process to what goes on in politics. It is rather governments that act like families, for where else did the human race learn to function like that?

This essay is divided into three major sections. Section I will discuss some effects of secrets on the emotional process of a family. Section II will, through specific examples, discuss some effects on families of revealing secrets. And Section III will add some thoughts about the ethics of not being "dependable" about keeping secrets.

I

I should like to begin with a short typology of family secrets.

+ Family member A gives information to member B and asks him not to tell members C–Z. For example, a son might tell his mother that he was arrested and ask her not to tell Dad.

+ A family, without making any conscious effort, has conspired to keep information closeted, such as the fact that grandma died by committing suicide and no one talks about it.

+ A third type of family secret, which is less obvious than the second, is one in which opinions or perceptions are accepted at face value and not checked out. For example, Dad tells his daughter how upset her mother is at the news she is getting married, and the daughter accepts this without ever speaking with Mom.

+ Finally, there is the secret that might be classified as the "unmentionable subject," such as the death of a six-year-old child twenty years ago, which is never discussed by the family

In all four cases, whether or not the information was intentionally kept secret or intentionally used to create binds, the effects on the family relationship system will be the same.

What are some of those effects? Here are the five that I believe to be most significant:

1. Distortion of perceptions and information, at the fact-gathering level.

2. Creation of pseudo-bonds and unnecessary estrangements.

3. Stabilizing of triangles and support for pathological family processes.

4. Dilution of family strengths.

5. Maintenance of anxiety at higher energy levels.

Effect 1. Distortion of Perceptions

This is one of the most elementary, far-reaching, and subtle effects of secrets on families. I start with this one because, after all, one's impressions, one's feelings, one's thoughts, one's behavior, one's theorizing is all based on the information one has obtained. To the extent that information itself is incorrect, one is dealing with what might be called secondary family process. By secondary family process I do not mean anything pseudo. Those feelings and behaviors are real and are having a real effect on the family members; but if they are based on misperceptions of reality seen dimly through a screen of obfuscation or outright lies, then root causes still in operation on a primary level may sabotage all efforts to get change in that secondary process level, making them always only temporary changes.

Whether one belongs to that part of the family that is in on or out of the secret, the basis of information upon which to act will be continually distorted by the continuing growth of assumptions that have emotionally committed themselves in a particular bias. Thus, on the one hand, secrets help maintain illusions; on the other hand, they prevent the admission of evidence contrary to one's fixed perception that might in a more open emotional climate change that very perception.

Effect 2. Creation of Alliances and Estrangements

Family secrets create alliances that produce bonds and binds as well as unnecessary estrangements. Effect #2 is, of course, a natural result of effect #1, the distortion of perceptions, but its manifestations are so strong and influential in their own right, they seem to deserve special mention. Clearly, how one perceives someone affects the kind of relationship one desires to have with him. But the secondary effects are extremely significant. There are children who never get to know their cousins, or divorced parents no longer living with them, or parents still living with them, because they have bought the perceptions of their parents or other emotionally significant members of the family. On the other hand, there are an enormous number of family relationships that maintain the strength they have only because a third member of the family has been distanced, triangled out, through secrets passed back and forth between those in the strong bond. This is obvious, for example, between mother and son when father is out of the information. Less obvious are the marriages maintained by creating an enemy in one of the in-laws. This happens of course when one spouse accepts as fact the opinions of the other spouse about his or her parents and never seeks to establish the kind of direct relationships that might produce contrary information. The couple, in other words, share a secret.

Effect 3. Stabilizing of Triangles

This a corollary of 1 and 2, or perhaps just a way of putting the first two more simply. Secrets in family life create triangles and help them to function. Secrecy in a family may be one of the most important internal forces in helping triangles to stabilize. Thus it may be said, family secrets *always* support the homeostasis of the family emotional system because openness and questions are inherently subversive. In fact, it may be a good rule of thumb that if you are on the side of change, then secrets work against you.[1]

Effect 4. Dilution of Strengths

Secrets in a family keep the family from functioning as an organized community. Family secrets seem to have an avalanche effect, dividing the community into parts and making it difficult for those on either side of the secret to communicate. And the important point here is that the difficulty in communication seems to spread out into all areas way beyond the subject of the original secret. In short, secrets in a family make it more difficult for that family to mobilize its natural strengths. For example, I once had to visit four sisters in the hospital after a severe automobile accident. Their kid brother had died, but the doctors did not want the sisters to know until they had recuperated more fully. I found myself unable to carry on any meaningful conversation, no less be of real comfort,

---

1. Though it should also be stated that the opposite phenomenon, someone who is incapable of keeping a secret, also stabilizes pathological processes.

as I had to be so careful about telling them the truth that I had to "pre-think" everything I was going to say to make sure it would not lead to some subject that might prompt them to ask a question about their brother.

Effect 5. High Anxiety

Secrecy in a family helps maintain anxiety at higher energy levels. This logically follows from the other four effects on communication, triangles, and perceptions. But two additional phenomena might be mentioned specifically here regarding trauma and diagnosis. I believe when a member of a family has gone or is going through a particularly disturbing emotional experience, the effects of the trauma will be prolonged and preserved by efforts of other family members who are aware of it and strive to keep it secret. When it is a child, secrecy surrounding the experience may itself make the experience traumatic. Regarding diagnosis, when members of a family receive a diagnosis about another member, whether it is a diagnosis regarding physical illness (say in a spouse or an elderly parent) or emotional difficulty (say a professional report about a child), keeping the information from that person will help fix a particular focus on that person and in turn will help maintain a higher energy level of anxiety about that person's condition and what they must be going through. I used to think people did not tell others bad news in order to spare their feelings; now I believe it is so they won't have to deal with their own feelings.

Actually, one of the keys to understanding how well the members of any family are able to differentiate themselves from one another may be the extent to which secrecy is used as a method for dealing with anxiety. I have been struck, for example, by the number of people I see where the impending death of a parent or other important person was kept from them, making me wonder to what extent that secrecy helped produce the problem they are now dealing with and to what extent it is just symptomatic of families that produce the kind of problems they were presently working on.

II

Now I should like to give some specific examples of the effects on a family when secrets are revealed. I will share four examples with you.

Two are from my own family and two are from clinical practice. The two from my own family are one in which I received a "revelation" and one in which I was the revealer. In one of the clinical practice examples I encouraged a client to reveal a secret in his family; in the other, acting as the therapist, I revealed secrets to all the members of a family I was seeing, which some members of the family had shared with me.

The first situation from my own family was rather deceptively simple. I am not sure exactly why, but it actually had great power. As a young only child growing up, I found myself constantly berated for not being a better boy. My recollection of my childhood in all events is that I was constantly in a state of disgrace, that is, out of favor, in guilt for again having done something mischievous. My father appeared to me to be a very good and clean person, quite conservative and always law-abiding. I had heard vague tales of his going off to join the navy during World War I before he was of age, but always attributed that to sheer patriotism. Several years ago, and long after his death, I had lunch with a cousin of his who had been his contemporary and whose older brother had been his playmate. In reminiscing she remembered the time her brother and my father were playing in her father's tailor shop and cut up the suit of a groom on his wedding day. I cannot begin to tell you the release I felt with the hearing of that information. I, of course, could hardly wait to tell my mother about it at the next opportunity and her reply was, and this is pretty close to an exact quote: "I never wanted you to know about those things when you were a child because I was afraid you'd wind up the same way."

I believe if you try to analyze the details of this whole situation too carefully, that is, what went into the keeping of my father's childhood secret, as well as the effect of the revelation of that vignette, you will miss the power involved in such family process.

In the second example from my family, my father's sister had been going downhill for several months, losing weight and becoming obsessed with fears that she had cancer. I had once seen a family in which as soon as the son, an only child, finally got closer to his wife than to his mother, the mother's heart went arrhythmic and she became convinced she had cancer despite the opinions of several medical experts to the contrary. I was beginning to suspect something similar was happening with my aunt because I had learned from her only son, my cousin, that he and his wife were terribly concerned about his hitherto adaptive, sweet daughter, now shacked up with a leftist admirer of Castro. He, of course, had revealed none of his concern to his prudish mother.

Around this time I had occasion to visit my cousin's daughter at a New England college. Shortly after I arrived and we began to discuss the family, my kid cousin mentioned almost matter-of-factly as a parenthesis in a sentence going somewhere else, "after I was raped." Donning all the cool scientific tone I could muster I asked, "Oh, when was that?" "Well," she said, "remember that birthday party you gave for your mother two years ago?" "Oh, yes," I said, "I remember." "Well, two days later when I was back in Cambridge where I was ushering in a playhouse for the summer, I walked home in a way that I really knew I shouldn't have, and it happened then." She added that I should please not tell any members of the family and that she wouldn't have even told her parents if it weren't for the fact that as a result of questions the police were asking she really needed their advice.

I would say that from the moment she told me, there was no question in my mind that I was going to tell her grandmother, my cousin's mother. But I wasn't sure of the best way. I began by confiding the secret to my mother, and she said, "If my sister-in-law ever heard that she would drop dead." Now I knew how to tell my aunt.

I wrote my seventy-six-year-old aunt that I had news that she would find very shocking and that my mother had said she would drop dead if she ever found out. I informed her that her granddaughter had been shacking up with someone and this was why her son, my cousin, was so upset about things. Then I added that what I had to tell her next was much worse. I informed her of the rape, immediately adding that her granddaughter had not become pregnant and that things seemed to be okay. I added that I thought her son needed her help because as an only son he wouldn't understand how girls felt about things like that, and also added that while the family thought she was a prude (my mother having told me once she thought she had been frigid in her marriage) that I was sure she could take it.

Upon receiving the letter my aunt phoned me to thank me and to tell me that this made a lot of things she sensed make sense. She still complains a lot about her health, but there has certainly been no deterioration during the past several years, as she reaches seventy-nine — or maybe it's eighty, she won't tell.

Also, my cousin who was raped and at that time was fused with her friend who made periodic trips to see Castro is now in her senior year of medical school.

One other point may be important to mention here. While finding out the truth may make people more upset, it reduces, I believe, their general level of anxiety. I don't think being upset has ever hurt anybody. I believe that anxiety kills.

The third example, one from clinical practice, involves my urging a client to reveal a secret in his family. The client was a professional man of about thirty living with a woman he had seriously considered marrying. He was Jewish; she was not. He had great fears about how his parents would react to the news that he loved, lived with, and might even marry a non-Jewish woman. He was unhappy about his relationships with each of his parents generally, and he had an older sister who used him as a confidant. Several years previously, in fact, the sister had told him that she had an operation on her back for a malignancy but made *him* swear never to tell Mom.

I suggested that he tell Mom when he brought his non-Jewish girl-friend up to meet them. My general experience in these situations has been that all attacks by parents on the marital choice of their children are red herrings, and that they stop almost miraculously if what is really bothering the parents in the system can be found and focused upon in-stead. He kind of let it slip out early on that weekend in front of his sister, who at first protested along with her husband that he had it wrong; it was a friend they were talking about who had the malignancy, but he innocently continued to press the point.

Some very interesting effects occurred. First, the parents never once mentioned the non-Jewishness of his fiancée throughout the weekend, nor have they made much of it since. And he reported that the following week after returning to the D.C. area *he* was functioning with much less over-responsibility for his paramour or the people in his work situation, which according to his perceptions was bringing positive results in both these areas.

He is continuing to work at the family relationship system, and it is my perception that many of his efforts would have had a more treadmill effect if the triangle between his sister, his mother, and himself had not first been *un*stabilized.

The fourth example involves my revealing to all the members of a family I was working with secrets I had become privy to in working with several of the members alone.

This was a family of four: an overfunctioning mother, who was a lawyer; a passive father, retired on a disability; and two sons, one thirty-one and one twenty-eight, neither of whom were functioning very well. The older son had originally come in with his wife. He was having an affair and was jobless after losing his position with a civil rights organization. The twenty-eight-year-old son, who was adopted, had not held a job for more than several months after getting out of the army several years previously. The parents were constantly "on" the adopted son, who lived with them, to shape up and become responsible, and were unceasing in their advice-giving efforts to the other son also.

The older brother often talked about the problems that the younger brother was having, particularly how he had gotten a fifteen-year-old black girl pregnant. Mother did know he was dating a black teenager and was very upset about it. I had, during the course of seeing him alone, suggested that he tell "cop-out" Father rather than Mother, which would have been his usual move. Discussion with the older brother also brought out the fact that Father had had an affair early in his own marriage. Then younger brother came in with older brother and talked about his difficulties in getting his parents off his back, so I suggested a session with the whole family. The parents had been in once before and opened this second meeting with: "I suppose this is going to be 'get the parents night' again. Why do you kids always blame us for everything?" Deciding that I was not interested in an evening of fighting denial over rather inconsequential issues, I responded: "Well, I must hand it to you both. I have never seen parents take things so calmly especially when they have two grown intelligent sons, neither functioning very well at work, one whose marriage has just dissolved, and the other having just knocked up a black girl."

Mother's response was to yell, "Oh, no," and to burst into tears, stand up, and start to walk out, but not very quickly. I suggested she stay and help the family open up. She stayed. Shortly afterwards I got around to asking Mother and Father what was going on in their marriage when Father had his affair. And lo and behold, it turned out that the adopted son had never known about that. A little later we somehow got on to Ibsen's play *Ghosts,* in which the father, an old roué, had VD, and the son, despite the mother's tremendous efforts, in a dramatic close to an early act, is seen going after the maid. And that reminded me to let out the fact that the adopted son now had VD. This did it for Mother. She got up again and left, while Dad, following her out, turned to me and said, "That was a low blow." The sons stayed a while and then left.

At the beginning of the following week, Mother called for a separate appointment. She had during the family session intimated some burden she had been carrying for twenty-eight years. What she told me was that while her younger son knew he was adopted, as did the whole family, she and her husband had kept the identity of his "real" parents secret: the natural mother of her adopted son was Father's sister.

At this point I dreamed I was in the middle of the last act of a Gilbert and Sullivan operetta and kept waiting for some foster mother or little Miss Buttercup herself to slip in and put everybody's past back in proper order. I quickly realized, however, that the mother in front of me was in fact the foster mother, and she would have to do the explaining. She took it upon herself to do just that, informing both of her sons: the adopted one that she was also his aunt, and his father his uncle, and her natural son that his brother was also his cousin.

Most important, however, is this. The older son, who was my original client, always had problems in even knowing what feelings he was trying to express. All efforts to work out problems were always taken on half-heartedly, and he seemed to have a light, denying veneer that he pasted over all his emotions. From that family session on he began to get in touch with himself, take himself more seriously, and make constructive moves towards his own growth. His parents, in turn, have pulled back into their own relationship. Younger son has moved out of the house, broken up with his adolescent girlfriend, and gotten a job in the same place as older brother, who now has risen to a position of responsibility. In terms of the integration of self that resulted for the older brother, I would say that the family secret-revealing session, if one can quantify such things, was worth a hundred analytic hours. In family terminology I would say that the effect of that session was to de-glob *him* from the undifferentiated mass of the system. The black teenager, by the way, aborted soon after this.[2]

---

2. Three years later, after the older brother had remarried and moved out of town, the parents, having retired and wanting to move to Florida, came back to work on the irresponsibility of the younger son.

In summary of this section on the effects of revealing secrets in families, I would like to say that I never cease to be amazed at the changes that follow such uncovering. It seems always to be much more than I would have predicted. That is, changes occur that apparently have nothing to do with the subject of the secret. And perhaps that is the most important point I could make. It is the fact of the *existence* of a secret, rather than its subject matter, that seems to affect the relationship system.

When secrets are revealed it is almost as though relationships deeply locked into one another in one particular way suddenly uncouple and are given an opportunity to recouple in different ways.

III

Finally, I would like to deal briefly with some of the ethical questions raised by not being "dependable" about keeping secrets, either in one's family or in one's office.

First of all, let me say that taking this approach has not come easily to me. I still do a lot of soul-searching about it, and as each new situation presents itself, despite my previous successful experience, I do it with heart in mouth.

When you "betray a confidence," as the expression goes, have you been a traitor to your family or your patient? Here is some of the thinking that has gone into the position at which I have arrived.

The management of information works both ways. I have decided that I am not bound to keep information secret if I am told it is a secret after I have been given the information. In other words, if someone tells you something and then says, "But promise me you won't tell anyone else," or "Don't tell X or Y," then they have in effect thrown a lasso around your neck and, with the request for silence, pulled the noose tight. It seems to me that what is *unethical* is to bind people with information or perceptions unless you have first asked them will they keep it secret, that is, are they willing to be lassoed?

In those situations where they ask for confidence first, before giving you the information, it would seem that the ethical thing is to say, "No, I can't keep a secret." I usually phrase this as, I feel I must be the judge of what I should do with information I have about the family. I am not going to run about as a tattletale but neither can I be bound to one member. I find most people are so burning to tell you the secret by that time they tell it to you anyway. And if they don't, you're still free, of course, to tell other members of the family that this one has a secret.

It is possible to argue that even if a member of a family has not gotten a prior commitment of confidence from you, that is their expectation because of the way psychotherapy and religious confession are practiced today. This seems to me to be a valid point. In actual practice, however, I have not found that point to matter much. I have almost never been attacked by a client for revealing a secret, if I can get the family to deal with it immediately. I believe this is true because I convey that my client is the family, and that I will be able to help the family best if I have no secret alliances with any of its members.[3]

Ultimately, however, my rationale for revealing secrets is pegged to two other ideas, one practical and one philosophical. The practical one is simply that I believe that when I engage in keeping confidences with certain members of the family from other members of the family, I am at the worst helping that family to destroy itself and at the least making all my other efforts to help the family a thousand times more difficult. I am stuck on a level of what I have previously referred to as secondary family process.

The philosophical point is that I deeply believe in civil liberties and the rights of human beings to have free access to all those aspects of their environment that might make their own choices better informed. It is really rather illusionary to try to formulate an "I" position when it's not clear where you are standing. While some might think revealing secrets is playing God, I see keeping secrets as playing God, as acting with great presumption about what information is good for people to know. And my constant surprise at the effects on a family when a secret is revealed convinces me that revealing secrets can be a great humbler for the therapist, in terms of what he thought the problems and the causes were and what the proper direction should be.

I should like to conclude with one short story that illustrates my position. Last summer in Atlanta at a special seminar on death during a

---

3. Actually, my experience has been that the person to whom the secret is revealed is more likely to be critical of the therapist than the family member whose confidence has been "betrayed." But then killing the messenger who brings bad news is an old tradition. In all events, such anger suggests that the secret-keeper in the family, far from always being the "manipulator," may often be doing it for the one who doesn't want to know!

rabbinic conference I had been taking a strong position about the importance of openness in the face of death. One of my colleagues who disagreed with my position on openness gave as an example a woman in his congregation whose husband was killed suddenly in a 75 mph head-on crash. He had to be the one to tell her. While he was there, the family doctor arrived, said he had seen the body at the morgue, and added, in comfort, that she may be reassured, he was barely scratched. My colleague went on to say that he saw no need to tell her the truth about what a 75 mph head-on crash would do to her husband's body. Perhaps now, two years later, as she was fully recovering from the trauma and again thinking of taking her place in society, she might be ready for the full truth — which she is probably beginning to admit to herself anyway. And my colleague turned to me and said, "What possible need could there have been to be open with her before this?"

My answer to him was, "You wasted two years of that woman's life."

About a year after this paper was delivered I was able to apply ideas originally conceived in its preparation to a situation I was quite familiar with in my own family. My mother had always told me that I was born with a spasmodic muscle in my stomach. Since I knew that my grandfather had been dying of leukemia during that period I imagined my symptom had something to do with my mother's upsetness over his condition. Though I always wondered why she had been so upset — everyone does die, after all. The impression I had always gotten was that my condition lasted for about the first year of my life. Then one day she happened to mention that it lasted for eight months. That was exactly the period of time my grandfather lived after my birth. In other words, my stomach got better right after be died! And then it hit me. They had never told him he was dying. That's why my mother was so upset during the terminal stage. I immediately called and asked her if my grandfather knew he was dying. "Of course not," she replied. "Throughout the whole two years he had it?" I pressed. "Naturally," she responded. "He was such a gentle man, we never could have done a thing like that."

Three

HOW TO SUCCEED IN THERAPY
WITHOUT REALLY TRYING

My approach as a therapist has been shaped at least as much by what I've observed outside the domain of therapy as by anything I've seen in my consultation room. I've spent much of my life trying to promote change in one way or another. I started out as a garden-variety Reform rabbi who was dismissed by my congregation after five years for conduct unbecoming a suburban clergyman, i.e., considering education more important than the building fund, and social action more significant than being social. I lasted two and a half years as a community relations specialist for the White House in the early 1960s, trying to help urban communities develop their own plans for integrated housing. I left when I realized that I was harboring ideas that were heretical for a civil servant, like the notion that getting things done now was more important than waiting till after the election, even if that meant upsetting the political applecart.

Preparing this essay has forced me to examine closely just how I approach my clinical work after nearly twenty years of being a family therapist. I anticipate that some may regard what I am about to say as indicating a deep pessimism regarding human nature, perhaps even an uncaring attitude towards my clients, but the fact is that I am as excited by doing therapy today as I was when I conducted my first session. I have had no struggles whatsoever with "burnout," that seemingly ubiquitous scourge of modern-day professionals. And while I never take my clients' anxiety home with me, I seem to have a clearer sense of personal fulfillment than I perceive in many of my colleagues who are far more

First published in *Networker* (May–June 1987): 27ff.

"involved" with their clients — and far more caught up in perseverative attempts to bring about change.

When I finally decided to become a therapist, my view about the conditions that promote change had already begun to develop. What struck me then and what has continued to impress me is how difficult it is to will fundamental changes in any social system, even when it is the best meaning, best educated, wisest members of the human species who are doing the willing. It has seemed to me that most efforts to bring about change anywhere wind up failing. Actually, the most profound changes I have witnessed are those that no one seems to have intended or predicted.

If one remains a clergyman in the same community for almost fifty years, as I have, one gets to watch an entire generation go by. Children whose bar mitzvahs I officiated at when I first came to Washington today have kids graduating college. I've not only done weddings (and funerals) for children whose parents I married; I've also done the second-time weddings of the divorced parents of those kids. I've seen many families change without going into therapy and many families fail to change despite decades, and I mean *decades,* of seeking help.

While being in therapy undoubtedly helped many families in my congregation through difficult periods in their lives, it would be hard for me to say that many of them changed in any fundamental way. Few seemed able to become more flexible in handling distance and closeness in their relationships or in becoming less anxious in the face of crisis or developing less victim-like attitudes towards life's setbacks. Similarly, as I look back at how kids have turned out over the years, there was no way I could have predicted their life course based on their early functioning and certainly not on the basis of how their parents raised them. Many of the most outstanding teenagers I knew have wound up deeply troubled, while many of the most troubled and troublesome have really taken off. I have never found any clear correlation between what society says makes good parents and how kids eventually turn out.

The evolution of the larger institutional systems I've observed over the past thirty years — whether religious, educational, medical, or governmental — has followed a similarly enigmatic course. In fact, I cannot think of any institution that I am familiar with that is functioning any more effectively today than when I first encountered it, despite changes in its leadership, policy, the economy, or progressive advances in the racial and gender mix of its employees. My guess is that the success rate among business consultants trying to change these large systems is no greater than that of family therapists trying to change families.

It seems to me that whether one is viewing the macrocosm (society) or the microcosm (the family), most of the changes that take place in social systems involve minor alterations rather than fundamental transformations. Further, few important changes follow from a deliberate act of will. I believe my survival as a therapist — by which I mean the fact that I am just as fascinated by the process of therapy today as when I conducted my first session — has to do with how I came to grips with the capacity of social systems of all sizes to absorb those who try to change them.

The Other Side

There is, of course, another side to the portrait I am painting of a world in which fundamental change is so unusual. During the past thirty years, we have all lived through a time of profound changes. Here are three brief vignettes of striking changes — one social, one political, and one from our own field — that stand out for me.

• I will never forget a recent visit to a South Carolina town that back in the 1960s had fought bitterly against blacks and whites even using the same drinking fountains. My first night I went to a restaurant and found it filled with interracial couples. But that was not the greatest shock. What was everyone eating in this one-time bastion of the Deep South's resistance to any alteration of its tradition? Sushi!

• The McCarthy era is now notorious for the hysteria that gripped public opinion and the way people's careers were destroyed because of "undesirable associations." One of my closest friends is a lawyer who defended all kinds of unpopular causes, including the Hollywood Ten, in the worst witch hunts of the early 1950s. Then in the 1970s, just before Watergate broke, Charles Colson joined his law firm. Being on the blind side of justice, my friend took his new partner's case when Colson became involved in the investigation. When my friend tried to counter the pre-judging efforts of the local press, he suddenly found many of his long-term, liberal friends refusing to associate with him.

In the midst of that, I said to him, "Things really have turned around, haven't they?" "Hell, no," he responded, "I'm still on the same side."

• When I first entered the field of psychotherapy a generation ago, family therapy was, at best, an obscure elective in social work schools. I decided to launch myself by sending a letter to physicians in my community announcing that I was going to start a counseling and consultation service. My naive idea was to help people find sources of counseling, the field then being so unfamiliar to the average lay person. I was immediately reported to the State Board of Medicine for conduct unbecoming a lay person. The charge, in fact, was that I was guilty of practicing medicine. The ostensible upset was that I had used the word "diagnosis" in my brochure (ironically a word I would never have used a few years later), and the act of diagnosing, according to some members of the local medical society, was a medical activity.

I tried, at first, to point out to the blue-ribbon committee selected to meet with me and my attorney that every Sears in town had a diagnostic center, but to no avail. Eventually, they agreed over a bottle of Jack Daniels to let me alone, if I would only stop using that word, and, of course, the brochure that contained it. Several years before, the first president of the American Association of Pastoral Counseling had been similarly challenged by the local psychoanalytic society because he had people lie down on a couch during therapy. That conflict was also resolved by compromise; he agreed only to do therapy with people when they were sitting up.

All this may sound absurd today at a time when analysts, representing an ever smaller percentage of therapists, seem like an endangered species. (These days they even submit papers for presentation at AAMFT conferences.) Today their *chutzpa* at trying to corner the market in therapy seems a bit ludicrous. But back when that was happening no one could have envisioned in his wildest dreams that the psychoanalytic dominance of the therapy world would decline so precipitously.

Each of these vignettes touches on the basic paradox of change. Despite human beings' extraordinary ability to maintain the status quo, the world keeps throwing the unanticipated developments our way that sometimes thwart our extraordinary talents for resisting change. For professional helpers the important point is that the more deliberately intended the attempt to bring about change, the more easily the resistance demons are triggered.

Mentors

In my own training, I was fortunate in having two mentors who understood as well as anyone I've ever met the folly of trying to will change. My first supervisor was Les Farber, a training analyst with the Washington Psychoanalytic Institute, who had an existential rather than an interpretive emphasis. For Farber, the central issue in therapy was distinguishing between what could be willed and what couldn't. For example, one could will sitting at the dinner table, but not appetite; one could will going to bed, but not sleep. (And I would add family members can will being together, but not togetherness.) Farber's view was that almost all neuroses and psychoses are a disorder of the will. The failure to accept the inescapable limitations of conscious control led to willing one's own thoughts (compulsivity) or one's environment, including others (hysteria).

Farber believed that it was not only patients who had disorders of the will. He taught me that helpers can fall into the same traps, believing that they could will their patients to think the way they'd like them to. Ultimately, Farber took the position that ineffective therapy — and also therapist burnout — come out of trying to will too much in the therapeutic relationship. Eventually, I came to realize that in almost all unsuccessful cases, the family therapist has been locked into a conflict of wills with his or her patients that is *identical* to the struggle of wills the family members are engaged in with one another.

Though Farber was not a family therapist, over the years I discovered that his views on willfulness could be applied productively to a system as well as an individual. The most serious symptoms in family life, e.g., anorexia, schizophrenia, suicide, always show up in families in which people make intense efforts to bend one another to their will. Indeed, over the years I've come to see that it is the presence or absence of willfulness that determines the extent to which any initial, abnormal behavior in a family will become chronic. And I have learned that the key to most cases is getting at least one member to let go of their willfulness.

The Dilemma of Change

All of this raises a crucial question. If our professional task is to bring about change, how can we avoid willing it? Farber's solution was to emphasize the difference between expressing one's own talents and desires versus achieving one's ends by trying to control and manipulate others. This is a distinction my other mentor, Murray Bowen, was to echo in his contrast between an "I" position and a "you" position or what he calls "no-self" behavior. Being supervised by Farber first and later Bowen in the late 1960s and early 1970s, a time dominated by the Vietnam conflict, I learned the madness of thinking that the therapist could prevail in a contest of wills. They taught me that no matter how many bombers you thought you had as a therapist, you could never overcome the Vietcong lurking in the tangled jungle of the client's resistance.

Since Farber left Washington a year after I began supervision with him, I'm not sure how much more influence he would have had on me had he stayed. I do know that I was more drawn to Bowen's clinical approach because of a critical difference I perceived between the two men. For all his brilliance and insightfulness, I found Farber too serious. There was a kind of mischievous quality to Murray that intrigued me. Farber was always straight (perhaps that was his willfulness), whereas Bowen seemed far less "principled." And I liked the irreverence implicit in fighting fire with fire and being devilish in the face of the satanic.

If Farber's notions of willfulness helped me understand the ineffectiveness of most initiatives for change, whether in families or in other types of institutions, Bowen's emphasis on the nonanxious presence helped me understand how to function in a nonwillful manner. As a born and bred Manhattanite, the only way I knew how to get things done was fast and aggressively. I was thus fascinated by how this "country hick" seemed to be able to take the "city slicker" every time. It was clear that he had heard it all before and was not going to be seduced by others' efforts to get him to change them.

There is a story about Bowen when he was running his famous project at NIMH, hospitalizing the families of schizophrenics, that illustrates the way he operates. A schizophrenic known for her repeated threats of suicide came to him one day requesting a weekend pass and also a prescription for sleeping pills.

Passive-Aggressive Therapy

I once heard someone say that Bowen practices passive-aggressive therapy, and there is something to that. The passive-aggressive position is, "I'm going to frustrate you without appearing to do so." Bowen's message to his clients is, "You can try and change me, but I'm going to frustrate your goal. No matter what you do, I will not be responsible for you." He believes that if one can maintain a nonanxious presence in any system, that very style of functioning in itself will have a beneficial systemic effect, *no matter what the problem.* His goal is always to keep the motivation for the outcome of treatment where it belongs and never take on responsibility for providing change.

Since I was used to thinking that the way to change is to "point out" problems, or give suggestions, Bowen's approach to change at first did not appear forceful enough. But I began to realize that far from being passive, refusing to supply the motivation or take the anxiety actually reduces the power of those patients who call the shots by trying to get people to change. Bowen's special insight was that the resistant client was dependent on the effort to change him and that it was possible to get that dependency working *for* the therapist rather than against him. Ultimately, Bowen's message was: "I will take responsibility only for what happens *in* the session, not between sessions; I will not be intimidated by the anxiety of my clients; I will force their own pain to be the motivating force for change."

The vehicle for change in Bowen's approach is not in the therapist's directives or interpretations, but in his questions. Again, if one thinks the way to bring change is to offer solutions, this might sound simply Rogerian, or perhaps even a cop-out. But that misunderstands the extraordinarily active role of questions in subverting mindsets, and the enormous amount of energy it takes to formulate challenging questions in the face of an aggressive onslaught of helplessness and dependency. Besides, who says you have to ask questions that are unloaded, or that you can't ask one member of the family a question you want another member to hear? So, faced with a couple in which a wife seemed anxiously defensive, constantly afraid of her husband's disapproval, Bowen's approach would be to turn to the husband and say, "Can you make your wife defensive anytime you want?"

The Human Phenomenon

I once heard Bowen say, "I think I did my best work with my research families." That comment had a remarkable effect on me. It was as if in one short remark he had caught it all. I realized that change comes best when it isn't the primary purpose of the encounter, but a *byproduct* of something else. For Bowen, that something else is his fascination with learning about life, what he calls understanding the "human phenomenon."

Given my experience with nonchange in the face of society's tremendous efforts, and the power of multigenerational emotional processes to recreate old patterns, Bowen's offhanded remark concisely expressed a whole philosophy and even a methodology for promoting change in a nonwillful way. When the therapist's primary concern is understanding the human condition, a natural patience emerges that enables one to outwait the resistance demons that, like the swiftest horses, can beat humans only over a short course. Such an attitude also provides an automatic regulator of the therapist's own anxiety since if you genuinely want to learn, you must not be willful about life, but rather let it teach you. That means you try not to interfere too much with what you are observing, except in a manner that will bring it more into relief. Maintaining the stance of a learner also helps foster the right distance so necessary for permitting growth in others, obtaining objectivity about what is happening, and keeping clear the distinction between symptoms and underlying emotional processes. For all these reasons, I saw the "research approach" as the secret to remaining connected in a nonanxious way. When the task of the clinician becomes learning about life rather than imposing change, the challenge of therapy lies no longer in the contest of will with the client, but in satisfying one's own curiosity about what makes people tick.

Over the years I've developed a special way of keeping myself focused on this task. In every session I use a yellow legal pad with a line drawn down the center of each page. To the left I write down anything having to do with the session in progress, e.g., a comment a client makes that I want to go back to, a thought or perception I would like to share later, some data that I consider significant for understanding this particular family. On the right side, I jot down every idea about life that comes into my head during a session. It might be an example of something I have been working on, or perhaps I say something in a more concise or better articulated way than I ever had before, or sometimes the client says something profound or witty that I would like to retain. And then every few weeks I go through my notepads and throw away the left side containing the specifics about the clients. It is the right side that keeps me learning and growing and that ultimately makes me a healthy presence in my clients' lives. Following this procedure is like putting all my client families into one large multiple family group. Whatever I learn from any therapeutic encounter is fed back to the others, with the result that all my clients learn from one another.

I am after one thing, no matter what the symptom — promoting differentiation throughout the system. This takes me totally out of the willful position of assuming I know what choices are best for my clients. For me, symptoms are not an enemy to be eliminated but pathways that lead me in my quest to understand the system. And I assume once people begin to differentiate themselves, symptoms will atrophy.

The Therapist's Role

At this stage in my career I've achieved some clarity about what my role is in the process of change. I believe that my effectiveness as a therapist has very little to do with any technical expertise or specialized knowledge. In fact, I don't think becoming an expert therapist has to do with the content of one's store of knowledge, but with the effect of the knowledge in making one a little less anxious. Further, I believe that the whole notion of "healing" others (no less "curing" them) is the most willful notion among helpful professionals. If it is to mean anything beyond symptom relief, healing *must be* a self-regenerative process. A physician does not sew your cells back together. Healing is promoted only by reducing the inflammation, encouraging the body's own sources of defense and replenishment, and sometimes challenging them, as with an inoculation. I try to conceive my role similarly as one whose presence can promote healing, not as one who heals.

The more I've moved away from my early rabbinical training, the more I've realized how much it has shaped how I see the therapist's job. In the *shtetls* of Eastern Europe, people went to see the "rebi" not because of his learning or intelligence or his worldly know-how. They went to him for his wisdom, the cumulative experience that had shaped the way he saw life and dealt with its adversities. That still seems to me the best way of understanding what therapists ultimately offer those who come to them for help.

Four

THE MYTH OF THE SHIKSA

Here is part of a letter that a Jewish mother sent to her son after learning that he really intended to marry the non-Jewish woman he had been dating:

> Dear Herbie.
>
> Well, if you want to commit suicide, I guess there is nothing I can do. But I can't tell you how much this shiksa business is hurting your father and me. I don't know if you realize that this will hurt us financially. We will probably have to leave town, and I will certainly have to give up my job teaching Hebrew. . . . Your father is sick over this — you know he hasn't been well. All I can say is that if he dies, I will hold you responsible.
>
> Mary may say that she loves you, but have you told her that we Jews think of Jesus as an illegitimate son?
>
> Love,
Mother

For a thousand years Eastern European Jews and their descendants have used the term *shiksa* to refer to a non-Jewish woman who lures Jewish men away from religion and family. This attractive will-o'-the-wisp, as folk imagination would have it, is seductive, immoral, ignorant, and insensitive to Jewish values. It is not just that she is unsuitable to the warmth of traditional Jewish family life — she will destroy it!

There can be no question that within the Jewish ethnic community intermarriage has long been perceived as a major threat to the survival of the Jewish people and their way of life. Experience with more than

This essay is adapted from Monica McGoldrick, John K. Pierce, and Joseph Giordano, eds., *Ethnicity and Family Therapy*, 1st edition (New York and London: The Guilford Press, 1981).

two thousand Jewish-Gentile marriages and the reactions of their families has taught me, however, that when it comes to the individual Jewish
family, this idea of the shiksa is myth. More important, the false assumptions that support it are hardly confined to Jewish families alone.
Such false assumptions are just as prevalent in cross-cultural marriages
of any combination, and they even appear in the families of culturally
compatible unions.

Precisely, therefore, because the myth of the shiksa and its constituent
myths are so bound up with one another, revealing the falsehood in the
particular automatically leads to revealing the truth in the universal. It is
the purpose of this essay to expose the myth of the shiksa in its specific
form — the way it surfaces in Jewish families — and, as a byproduct,
to extract some new ideas about the general relationship of family and
culture. Regarding the particular, I will show how matters such as which
Jews are most likely to be "seduced," which families and which members
of those families are most likely to be reactive, and what strategies maximize keeping those families together all can be understood as matters of
family process rather than culture. Then, broadening the perspective, I
will show, first, how family process universally wraps itself in the garb of
"cultural camouflage" and, second, how focus on background factors by
families of any culture, as well as their therapists, supports an unwilling
conspiracy of denial.

Clinical Experience

The ideas and examples to be presented here are based on twenty-two
years of continuous experience in the cosmopolitan and international
setting of Washington, D.C. During these decades, this area became a
"mecca" for people from all over our planet and thus a fertile seeding
ground for the cross-pollination of love.

Throughout this period as both a rabbi with a specific responsibility within the Jewish ethnic community and a family therapist with a
broadly ecumenical practice, I found myself with an unusual opportunity to view cross-cultural marriage and family reactions within both
particular and universal settings. As this situation developed, my position became one of reciprocal feedback. On the one hand, my growing
awareness of the universality of family process that had been tutored

by my experience with non-Jewish families helped me get past the cultural myths within Jewish families. Then, as I began to understand the emotional processes behind the cultural myth I was observing in Jewish families, I was able to carry that understanding back to all families as universal principles. Eventually I came to see the myth of the shiksa as a prototype, but for two decades it was my laboratory.

I first began to think about the relationship between culture and family process when I tried to understand a paradox about Jewish-Gentile marriage. In my premarital counseling, first, I found that Jews who married non-Jews were not at all uninterested in the survival of their ethnic community, which was contrary to what the community assumed. Second, I noticed that many of the relatives who phrased their opposition to such a marriage in terms of concern for Jewish survival had not themselves led lives evidencing such concern and had become defenders of the faith overnight. Third, and most surprising to me, was the fact that over and over I found the grandparents, though usually more traditional than the parents, generally were more accepting.

Next I began to see that there were significant correlations between the ideological positions individuals took on such marriages and their positions in their family. This seemed to be true both about which child "married out" and which family member reacted most strongly. Back in the late 1960s, I began to report these findings at symposia of family therapists. Almost unanimously their response confirmed my perceptions. More than that, many began to refer to me mixed couples where neither partner was Jewish, for example, Protestant-Catholic, black-white, Greek Orthodox–Russian Orthodox, European-Asian, Japanese-Chinese. In all, the number of different combinations probably reached fifty.

These referrals gave me the opportunity to realize that certain family emotional phenomena that I had found to be true about Jewish-Gentile mixed marriages — for example, which child in the family tended to intermarry and who threatened to have a heart attack at the wedding — were just as true regarding mixed marriages where neither partner was Jewish.

I then began to see mixed couples in the same counseling groups. Here I found that blacks and whites, Turks and Greeks, Russians and Japanese, Puerto Ricans and WASPs, and Germans and Jews could gain as much insight into their own families from observing the emotional processes of these "other" families as from observing families of a similar cultural milieu, sometimes more. At the beginning of these sessions I was so caught up myself in the general mythology surrounding culture and family process that I was astounded by the similarity in the emotional processes between non-Jewish and Jewish family life.

Eventually, the uniqueness of my position in the Jewish and non-Jewish worlds began to pay off. I was able to develop a new hypothesis about the relationship between culture and family process that helped explain and integrate everything I was observing.

My hypothesis, which is the basic premise of this chapter, is as follows: Rather than supplying the determinants of family dynamics, *culture and environment supply the medium through which family process works its art.* Culture and environment may contribute to the morphology of a family's symptoms, but they do not determine which families or which individuals from which families in a given culture are to become symptomatic. Rather than determining family dynamics, culture and environment *stain* them; that is, they make them visible. It is not that sociologists and anthropologists are wrong in their descriptions of various kinds of family life. What is wrong is to assume that any family, at any given time, is beleaguered by relational conflicts *because* of its culture or environmental setting, even when the family issues are directly related to these factors. In certain situations culture and environment can tip the balance, of course, but, generally, their effect on a given family's emotional processes is not so much to shape them as to supply the fabric for their design.

A simple test of the relative significance of culture and process in understandings the emotional functioning of any family is as follows. Cultural and environmental factors can no more be the sufficient or the necessary conditions for the creation of pathology in a society than paint and canvas can produce artistic accomplishment. Thus even if we could know all the cultural and environmental factors in a given family's background, we could still not posit the future of that family's health. On the other hand, if we could know all the dynamics of that family's emotional heritage and not know anything about their cultural and environmental background, we could posit the future of that family with a high degree of accuracy.

Elsewhere I have shown that it is possible to isolate the family emotional process as a force independent from cultural background by describing ten rules of family process regarding distance, chronic conditions, symptom formation, cutoffs, secrets, pain thresholds, sibling position, homeostasis, and diagnosis, which have the same validity for all families irrespective of cultural background. This hypothesis should not be seen in any way as an effort to minimize or refute the general importance of ethnic and cultural values and customs in the enriching, developing, and stabilizing of family life everywhere. The emphasis here, rather, is that those same very important factors that ordinarily contribute mightily to the creation of a family, under certain conditions, are used to disguise what is destroying the same family. Ironically, as a rabbi committed to the survival of my people I came to find that I could often further positive feelings about being Jewish through approaches aimed primarily at waning the intensity of a family relationship system, even when, paradoxically, those very approaches seemed to be almost on the opposite side of reinforcing cultural commitment.

It is the failure to appreciate how emotional processes are camouflaged rather than determined by culture that enables family members to blame the background of others as the source of their discontent and their inability to change. Cultural camouflage encourages family members everywhere to avoid taking personal responsibility for their own points of view. It may be worse. The constant focus on and interminable discussion of background factors either among family members or with family members and their counselors allow important emotional forces to operate in their pernicious way, undetected.

It is only when we can see culture as a stain rather than a cause of family relational problems that we can devise appropriate strategies for affecting the underlying emotional processes that, rather than the cultural factors or differences themselves, have the real power to destroy that family or keep it together.

This essay is organized into three sections that follow the course of my experience. The first section will describe how ethnic cultural mythology operates in Jewish family life. The second section will show how Jewish families were helped to deal with potentially family-splitting crises when the underlying emotional "demons" in these families lost their cultural masks. The third section will develop the ideas of the first two sections into universal principles about the relationship of culture and family process in all families and then show how those principles feed back to even deeper understandings of the myth of the shiksa in Jewish families.

Ethnic Mythology and Jewish Family Life

The most blatant aspect of the myth of the shiksa today is that she will, or even wants to, attract a Jewish man away from his origins, no less destroy his family. In my experience that is the last thing she wants, generally being attracted herself to that very rootedness that she often lacks. Indeed, if there does exist a "shiksa" today, she is to be found, of all places, among Jewish women. For, in my experience, it is far more likely that when Jews and non-Jews marry it will generally be the non-Jewish partner who is influenced away from his or her origins. When the focus is confined to those marriages in which the Jewish partner is female, then I have to add that I have almost never seen such a union where the non-Jewish male will be the less adaptive partner in family matters.

The myth of the shiksa within the Jewish community today is thus doubly misleading. Not only are the designs of the non-Jewish woman who marries a Jewish man generally towards the preservation of his background rather than its destruction, but that same preservation instinct in Jewish women who marry non-Jewish men generally puts them in the very position that the term shiksa was originally intended to describe, that is, a woman who will seduce her man away from his background.

How then shall we account for the extremely negative reactions, some of them almost psychotic, that can occur in Jewish families when they find out who's coming to brunch? It is possible to answer this question with some conventional sociological theory. We might say that although times have changed, there is a lag in the perception of any minority group that is concerned about its own preservation. Given the experience of the Holocaust, the military threats to the state of Israel, and the long history of deep concern for survival, the Jewish people are naturally going to be even more xenophobic.

In my experience, the problem with such thinking is that I have never been able to find any necessary correlation between the degree of sociological or psychological sophistication in a Jewish family and how they respond to a mixed marriage. Nor have I found that a correlation necessarily exists between past exposure to threats to the Jewish people and how they respond to a mixed marriage. If a family that survived the Holocaust gets upset it is natural to say, "We can understand, given their past." If a deeply assimilated family from an old, established southern Jewish community is accepting, we may be prone to explain, "What do you expect, given the diluting of Jewish identity in their background?" The problem with these background explanations is that I have often seen survivors from the Holocaust not react negatively, saying, "We have had enough turmoil in our lives," and, on the other hand, I have often seen so-called assimilated fathers take to bed for weeks.

Nor, as my experience increased, did it become possible to predict how any parents might react based on information such as the size of their town, their section of the United States, their degree of Jewish education or synagogue attendance, the amounts they gave to the United Jewish Appeal, or their trips to Israel per year. Clearly, something deeper than cultural background or lag supported the myth of the shiksa. Something else had to be present to modulate the ethnic material. A history of cultural commitment simply was not sufficient to create the reaction, and in some cases it did not even seem necessary.

My first clue to the missing variable came from observing the other side of the issue, namely, who in which Jewish family was most likely to marry an outsider. Here also I found that the commonsense wisdom did not offer adequate explanation. While broad statistical studies might show inverse proportion between mixed marriage and cultural background factors such as keeping kosher, synagogue attendance, and the number of Jewish books in the house, there were too many exceptions when it came down to the specific Jewish families in which mixed marriages were occurring. If deep commitment for Jewish values and customs prevented or inhibited mixed marriage in many situations, why did it not have the same prophylactic effect in many other families? None of the usual assumptions about the degree of Jewish education and the inculcation of values necessarily held up. In fact, the correlations linking Jewish values and mixed marriages were skewed further. For it often seemed that the cultural background factors had worked and not worked at the same time. Over and over, I found that the Jewish partners who came from a family with a strong cultural tie felt intensely Jewish despite their decision to marry a non-Jew. *In their own minds one seemed to have nothing to do with the other.*

Finally a factor did begin to show up, a variable that seemed to be more determinative than cultural influence. It did not explain in every single case which Jewish individuals became candidates for cross-cultural marriage, but it seemed particularly important because it also helped to explain why the intensity of family reactions was not necessarily proportional to the degree of cultural commitment. It put both sides of the issue together in a new way, and as things turned out, it eventually led to effective strategies for family harmony.

I began to realize that Jews who married non-Jews overwhelmingly occupied the sibling position of oldest, or only, with only child defined as an actual single child or any child where there was a gap of five or more years between siblings. Such a correlation, I knew, could have meant that they simply exhibited the pioneering or leadership attribute frequently found in individuals from that sibling position. I soon learned, however, that this unusual correspondence between sibling position and the "insider" who married an "outsider" was a hint of something far more significant, something that could be true even when the insider did not occupy that particular sibling position.

As a family therapist who had taken thousands of multigenerational family histories, I knew that the child occupying the sibling position of oldest or only tended to be the focused or triangled child.

As is well known, a major and convenient way that some marital partners reduce the stress and intensity of their own relationship is by tuning down the overall emotional potential in their marriage by siphoning off the excess emotion onto the child. Such a child naturally becomes more important to the balance of the parents' relationship than his or her siblings, and where the resulting balance of the marriage is a calm and seemingly perfect fit, the importance of the child to its balance may not even be realized.

The child most likely to be emotionally triangled in this way does not always occupy the sibling position of oldest or only, of course. The child tends to be either an only, by the nature of things, or a firstborn simply because he or she was the only one around when the parents' marriage was in its early stages of formation as the parents disengaged from their parents. Any child can occupy this position if the timing is right, for example, when the parents' marriage needs rebalancing such as after a previously triangled child leaves (or dies) or the child is born close in time to the death of a grandparent who has been particularly important to one of the parents. Such a child, regardless of sibling position, might replace that grandparent in a similar emotional triangle that had helped balance the parents' marriage from the beginning.

In any event, if the child occupying such a position in the family does something that is perceived by the parents to be taking him or her out of that set of emotional interdependencies, the parents' anxiety will immediately increase. And it goes without saying that the triangled child will always have more difficulty leaving home!

I began to apply this hypothesis of the *triangled child* to Jewish families involved in mixed marriage, and many things came together. Not only did it help explain the inconsistencies between the degree of exposure to cultural influence and which family member married out or reacted most intensely, but it also helped explain who married further out, that is, interracially as well as interreligiously. For if parents generally have difficulty separating from the emotionally triangled child, the more intense the emotional circuits of that triangle, the more difficulty the child has separating from the parents. More powerful circuits need more powerful circuit breakers.

I thus formed the following hypothesis: *In any Jewish (or ethnic) family the child most likely to marry out is the child most important to the balance of the parents' marriage either right then or while growing up.* Further, the parent (or other relative) most likely to react negatively occupied a similar position in his or her own family of origin, either during childhood or right then.

It was, I decided, anxiety over the loss of a previously balanced togetherness that could suddenly turn the genes of cultural commitment on, as in the case of many reacting parents, or slowly off, as in the case of many offspring.

But still a piece was missing. For even if my hypothesis about family position rather than degree of cultural commitment was correct, why this kind of marriage in that kind of family? What was the connection between family process and cultural symptoms?

What I eventually came to learn was that in any family, but particularly in easily identifiably ethnic families, to the extent the emotional system is intense, members confuse feelings about their ethnicity with feelings about their family. The resulting inability to distinguish one from the other eventually leads to a situation in which reactions in the family relationship system are discussed with the vocabulary of the family's cultural milieu. I soon came to realize that focus on cultural background was a major way members of many Jewish families avoided focusing on their emotional processes.

The inadvertent yet all-encompassing nature of this phenomenon is illustrated by the following list of comments made by Jewish partners in my office. All were spoken in passing as someone was talking about family life back home or expectations about the future.

* I came from a typical Old World Jewish family in which Father was the boss.
* I came from a typical Old World Jewish family in which Mother was the boss.
* Jews don't talk about death.
* Boating is a Gentile sport.
* Jews don't live near forests.
* I thought Jewish weddings were buffet.
* Jews don't talk about sex.
* I thought Jewish weddings don't have place cards.
* You never can get Jews to be serious when they are eating.
* I thought Jewish weddings were always on Saturday night.
* Jewish families don't joke at dinner.
* I thought Jewish weddings always began when the minute hand was moving up the clock.
* Jewish girls always stay with their mothers.
* Jews aren't interested in watching sports on TV.
* Jewish boys can't get away from their mothers.
* In the Jewish religion we don't tell our ages.

- Why do I worry about him? I'm Jewish.
- My daughter reminds me of a shiksa — she's so cold and distant.
- Jewish women wear knit suits.
- My father was a typical Jewish father; you know, quiet, passive, let Mom do all the work in raising us.
- Jewish mothers are dirty fighters.
- I have a typical Jewish girl's build, small on top and big on the bottom.
- Jewish parents don't let their kids sit in the living room.
- Jewish parents don't take vacations without their kids.
- Jewish wives know how to train their husbands.
- Jews like contemporary homes.
- Jewish parents don't charge their daughters rent if they come home again.
- Jewish families don't make big deals over birthdays.
- Jews always buy discount.
- Distance is fundamentally a non-Jewish concept.

As I will show in the third section, this phenomenon is hardly confined to Jewish families or even to other ethnic families. The less intense the family, the less likely this is to happen. But a general principle does emerge, namely, that members of families, regardless of cultural background, are more likely to fuse cultural values and family processes when an important emotional issue has been touched or when the general level of family anxiety has increased.

In any event, once I began to defocus culture in my work with mixed couples and to pay less attention to the ethnic words, customs, and rubrics usually used by Jewish families to explain intermarriage and personal reactions, a harvest of insights accrued, both about the myth of the shiksa specifically and about the relationship of family and culture generally.

There is one more emotional aspect of ethnicity that needs to be mentioned before showing the therapeutic efficacy of bypassing cultural content.

An ethnic system operates like an extended family composed of nu-clear subgroupings. Anxiety in either the nuclear or extended system can escalate anxiety in the other. While this is true for any ethnic group, it has been particularly true about individual Jewish families in relation to what I would call the greater Jewish family (the worldwide Jewish community). Since the Nazi Holocaust and amid the constant threat to Israel, sporadic anti-Semitic incidents in various countries, the falling Jewish birthrate, and the generally lessened interest in synagogue mem-bership, the greater Jewish family is in a state of chronic anxiety about its survival.

The reciprocal elevation of anxiety between individual nuclear Jewish families and the extended system of the Jewish community works as follows: Members of an individual Jewish family concerned about the survival and togetherness of their own small group become more anxious about their personal family when they read or hear talk from community leaders about the survival and togetherness of the greater Jewish family. Similarly, when the leaders of individual Jewish families anxiously go to the community leaders for help over an issue such as mixed marriage (which in the minds of those family members has to do primarily with worries over their personal families, not worries about the community), the community leaders hear these reports as more proof that their family (the Jewish community) is in danger, and their overall anxiety increases.

This comparison of an ethnic community to an extended family is not inconsistent with the thesis that it is family process that counts, not culture. I am talking about the emotional processes in an ethnic commu-nity, not its cultural content. Of all the social groupings that act like a family, none is more like a family than an ethnic group, combining as it does all the same factors that make a family behave with the emotional intensity of a biological organism: genetic pool, long-term association, similar physiognomy, generations of emotional dependency, and so on.

The etymological history of the word "shiksa" itself is instructive of this relationship between a culture and its constituent families. The He-brew verb *shakaytz* means to abominate, to utterly detest. In the Bible there are constant admonitions not to eat or take the *shikutz* (masculine noun form), literally, "abominated thing," into one's house. But why was it necessary to have laws designed to keep people away from that which is abominable? We find no laws today against taking garbage into the house. Obviously whatever the *shikuizim* (plural) were, they were not by nature abominable but were probably attractive and were given this term of opprobrium to dilute people's desire.

There is, by the way, no feminine form of the root *shakaytz* anywhere in the Hebrew Bible; that grammatical construction does not exist. Only in the Middle Ages, in Europe, does the term *shiktsa* (feminine form) begin to surface among the Yiddish-speaking Jews of the ghetto who, obviously hemmed in by their physical and other walls, found the apparent freedom of the non-Jew attractive. The psychology was the same, but the focus had switched from foreign holy objects to foreign (strange?) women.

Family Process and Cultural Costume

In this section I will show how it is possible to understand four basic aspects of the myth of the shiksa in terms of family process rather than culture and how such understanding can help Jewish families thrown into crisis over an impending mixed marriage. They are (1) which family member is most likely to be reactive; (2) what therapeutic strategies are most likely to reduce negative reactions and gain acceptance; (3) which families are most likely to be unaccepting; and (4) what variables have an influence on which given Jewish family is likely to have one of its members marry out.

The Reactive Relative

When some Jewish parents realize that they might have a non-Jewish in-law the reaction can be severe. I have seen Jewish mothers threaten suicide and Jewish fathers go into severe states of depression. I have heard of threats to cut children off emotionally and financially and to get the child kicked out of medical school! I have witnessed harassment in the form of daily letters or phone calls. I have seen parents resort to arguing the Jewish partner out of the potential marriage, and I have seen the effort made with the non-Jewish partner. Whatever form the reaction takes, however, the rationale is usually phrased in terms of, or accompanied by comments on, the survival of the Jewish people. "How can you do this to us?" is usually mixed with "Remember the Holocaust?" The personal qualities of the non-Jew will be attacked along with comments on the superiority of Jewish family life. It leaves the impression that the reacting relative is, if somewhat belatedly, terribly concerned about the survival of Judaism, or at least Jewish family life.

There are reasons for doubting this impression. First, I have only seen failure in efforts to change such reactive family members when the issues were discussed in philosophical or sociological terms of ethnic survival. Over and over, I have seen the Jewish partner go home for a weekend, explain his or her position logically and eloquently, return feeling much better about things, and then receive a letter showing that the parents are back at ground zero. The second problem with automatically assuming that cultural survival or purity is the real issue when it is invoked at such intense moments of family anxiety is the usual response of the grand-parents. As I have mentioned, I have almost never seen the grandparents (who are usually more traditional) react more negatively than their less traditional children, the parents. This finding has been so universal that whenever a bride or groom reports that a grandparent is upset, I always ask, "Did you get that directly or hear it from your grandparents' son or daughter?" (i.e., Mom or Dad). Invariably it was heard from the bride's or groom's parent. Time and time again I have found that the grandpar-ent is more accepting. But how could a leap-a-generation camaraderie overcome so basic an anxiety as in-group survival?

The degree of commitment to Jewish survival is almost irrelevant to the degree of reaction when a family member marries a non-Jew. What is relevant are the following three emotional coordinates of the react-ing family member. In other words, irrespective of the language used to phrase the reaction and irrespective of the degree of cultural commitment the reacting relative has shown in the past, the following three emotional factors are always present:

1. There is little distinction of self between the reacting relative and the person getting married. This is so much the case that the re-acting relative almost experiences the upcoming marriage as his or her own.

2. There are important issues that have not been worked out in the reacting relative's own marriage. In fact it may be generally true that individuals who are satisfied in their own marriages rarely react intensely to another's.

3. The reacting relative is always caught in some important emotionally responsible position in his or her own family of origin.

The third is really the most important, as I will show shortly, for devising
therapeutic strategies, and in some ways it makes the first two redundant.
For the former usually follow from the latter.

An objection at this point may be, "Surely this would not be true
regarding Orthodox Jews." First, that has not always been my experience. Beyond that, however, what is important for understanding and
changing the emotional processes in a family is not the cultural position
individuals take at such times but *how they function with that position.*
Even if it were true that an Orthodox Jew is more likely to object to a
mixed marriage (or for that matter an observant Catholic to marriage
to a divorcee), the intensity with which that relative reacts is another
matter, and that can tell much about the person's family and his or her
position in it.

For example, an objection simply stated as such or even a refusal to
go to an event because it is against one's principles can be understood
as a definition of position. On the other hand, cutting off, disinheriting,
constant harassment, saying "This will put a knife in my heart," heavy
interference at such moments has little to do with cultural values and
traditions, even though the family members who are acting that way
may claim their faith supports their behavior and even though at other,
less emotional times the same expressed concern for survival, purity,
and so on reflects positive commitment to and deep involvement in the
tradition. The roots of such fanaticism will be found in those family
members' unworked out relationships with their own family of origin.

For example, *shiva,* which means "seven," is the Jewish mourning period for a first-degree relative during which traditional Jews stay at home
for a week. Some Jews have "sat *shiva*" for a child who has married out,
literally cutting him or her off from the family. While this would appear
to be Jewish because the process is wrapped in a fundamental Jewish cus-
tom, nothing could be more misleading. Nowhere has the mainstream of
Jewish tradition suggested that this be done, and it is done today (ritually
or symbolically) by Jews who are ordinarily so nontraditional that they
probably would not go through the ritual of sitting *shiva* when a relative really dies. We have here a good example of the universal emotional

phenomenon I shall describe in the next section as the "neurotic usefulness of religious tradition." Family cut-offs are emotional, not cultural,
phenomena and always require the consent of the one cut off. Where
that individual will not consent, working on the emotional processes in
the cutting-off parent can eventually reconnect the two family members.

Therapeutic Strategies

What has substantiated in my own mind the accuracy of the matrix of
three previously motivated emotional factors has been the high degree
of success I have had in creating therapeutic strategies for change based
on their coordinates. Not only have I found that by ignoring the cultural
content of the reacting family member and focusing instead on the family
coordinates it is possible to affect the intensity of the reaction, but I have
found that focus on the family process also can affect the rigidity of the
ideological positions! It never works the other way.

Time and again I have seen a family member's most rigid, culturally based positions change when the emotional processes of that family
change. But I have never seen the emotional tone, quality, or attitudes
of family members change through a direct confrontation on ideological
or cultural issues. On the contrary, the latter approach intensified the
deeper emotional issues.

The approach I have taken with clients is, first, to help them defocus the cultural issue and, second, to address aggressively the emotional
processes that are producing the extreme reaction. Usually it is the bride
or groom who is the client. Where that is the case I have through a
combination of family history taking and straight teaching about family
process first tried to depersonalize the problem. By that I mean I have
tried to cut down the bride's or groom's reactivity to parents' emotion-
ality by showing that he or she is the focus of a process that usually goes
beyond even the parents.

I try to show how efforts to bring parents around, especially by discussing the content of the charges, only keeps the focus (displacement)
on the person. To the extent the bride or groom can understand this I
then make direct suggestions for interfering with the multigenerational
transmission process that is funneling its way down.

Where the parents are the clients and they have come in to stop the
child from "destroying" herself or himself, the goals are the same though

the techniques may differ, and the therapy has to be more subtle. I try to switch their goal from stopping the marriage or breaking up the relationship to getting better definition of self between them and their child, or I show how when other parents have succeeded in accomplishing this, their children usually respond by drawing closer and either breaking up the relationship themselves (sometimes even after marriage) or forcing the partner to grow. In the process, if the parents' focus can be switched to their marriage, or their own families of origin, the cultural issues tend to disappear. In short, procedures that can refocus the parents on their own marriage or involve parents more in their own extended systems have been successful in eliminating the cultural issues. And this has been true no matter how traditional the parents or the phrasing of their position.

I will give one example with respect to each of the emotional coordinates mentioned in the section "The Reactive Relative."

1. *Lack of differentiation between the reacting relative and the person getting married.* The general thrust here is to stay out of the "content" of the charges or the pathos of the martyrdom. Paradoxical and playful techniques have proven remarkably effective. For example, "How can you do this to us, after all we have done for you?" can be met with "Mother, why do I have so much power to hurt you?" "Doesn't Jewish survival mean anything to you?" can be met with "The problem is, Father, that you didn't keep kosher."

"Where did I fail?" can be answered with, "If you had sent me to Hebrew school more often this wouldn't have happened" and "We tried, but you wouldn't go" with "But you were the parent, you should have forced me." And it never hurts the process for the child to add, "If your mother were only here now!" Such comments, however, only bring breathing space; they do not result in lasting change, though they do reduce the intensity and the reactivity.

But emotional coordinate (1) is always a symptom of (2) and (3). It therefore follows that no matter what the focused issue between parent and child and whether or not it is cultural, dealing with coordinate (1) alone never brings lasting change. A fundamental shift occurs only by dealing with those coordinates that underpin it.

2. *Importance of the child to the balance of the reacting relative's marriage.* Parents who are satisfied in their own marriage do not react

with prolonged negative intensity to the marriage of one of their children. It follows that one of the most surefire ways of shifting the displacement from the child is to refocus the parent on his or her own marriage. For the mother-daughter relation, here is an example of a speech or letter that I have taught to brides as a way of accomplishing this shift:

> Mother, I know you are opposed to John, and you have a right to your position, but you are still my mother and I believe you owe me one more thing before John and I marry. We have never had a frank talk about sex. What has been the secret to your marital success? How many times a week would you say a man likes it? And when you don't want it, how do you keep a man away?

It is really remarkable how that paragraph will get mothers to cease their efforts to force-feed Jewish history.

Of course, not every daughter can do that little speech. So maybe the success I have seen with this one is that by selection, those daughters who can write it or say it are so well on their own way to disengagement that their own nonreactivity keeps them out of an escalating position, and without feedback to support it, the parents' reactivity wanes.

Whatever the reason, the basic point still holds: cultural positions are susceptible to change by dealing with the underlying emotional processes.

3. *The reacting relative is always caught in some important emotionally responsible position in his or her own family of origin.* Often the extended family of a reacting relative has not even been told that a son or daughter is marrying out because "This would kill my father." I once saw a situation where a mother, ordinarily obsessed with prestige, omitted from a newspaper announcement of her daughter's engagement the fact that her future son-in-law's family went back to the Virginia House of Burgesses, the well-known first legislative body in the United States, for such information would clearly have identified her daughter's future husband as non-Jewish.

I have found that if the bride or groom can outflank the reacting relative in his or her own family of origin, causing members of that family to interact with the parents, then even the most extreme reactions usually go quietly away. One way I have coached the bride or groom to catalyze this process is with a letter such as the one that follows, written preferably to the grandparent but sometimes to another family leader such as an uncle or aunt. That is, it must go to a parent or a peer of the parent.

> Dear Grand..., or Aunt, or Uncle,
>
> As you may have heard [they probably haven't] I am going to marry a non-Jew [a Catholic, a black, a Martian]. I would like to invite you to the wedding even though I know this probably goes so much against your principles that you may feel you can't attend. However, I did want you to know. Also, I wondered if you could give me some advice. Your daughter/sister (never "my mother") is absolutely off the wall about this. She keeps telling me this will be the end of our relationship, calls me every night, and says if you found out you would drop dead. I wonder if you could give me any information that would explain why she is behaving this way or any advice on how to deal with her.

Generally the letter writer does not even receive an answer, but the next time the bride or groom has spoken to his or her own parent, there is often a marked change. This approach has worked as well for non-Jewish as for Jewish families. It will work as well in the future when the first Alfa-Centurians arrive and earthling children are warned not to intermarry with creatures who grew up in a different solar system. For it will be the same kind of families that will react and the same kind of families that will produce intergalactic unions.[1]

The universal success of this approach supports, I believe, the basic premise that when it comes to intense moments in a Jewish emotional system, cultural issues are often red herrings, displacement issues that disintegrate when the emotional processes that spawn them are nullified.

---

1. When this essay was delivered in Tel Aviv, I suggested that in Israel, where there was not a plentiful supply of shiksas, the children of Jewish families who, had they lived in the United States, would have intermarried with non-Jews, would intermarry with Jews of extremely different backgrounds, for example, German Yemenite or Russian Iraqi. I was drawing on my experience that twenty years ago in the United States a high degree of emotional reactivity could get started even in an all-Jewish marriage from different backgrounds. In fact, there was a time when in some cities, Baltimore, for example, Jews of different backgrounds exclusively joined different country clubs. B'nai B'rith, created by German Jews, originally would not allow the admission of Eastern European Jews. In all events, the audience of Israeli therapists immediately informed me that since 1967, when Israel captured the West Bank, the plentiful supply of non-Jews had arrived and that an increasing problem there was Jewish women and Arab men. Their experience with these situations fit with my hypotheses.

Unaccepting Families

A third aspect of the myth of the shiksa that can be explained in terms of emotional process rather than culture is which Jewish families make the acceptance of an outsider contingent on conversion. While it is not always true, most reactive family members will accept an "outsider" if he or she converts. In fact, in some families, the immediate focus is conversion, with all efforts going in that direction rather than the direction of preventing the marriage from taking place, though there are situations where a Jewish family or family member will not accept a non-Jew even after properly constituted conversion. Scrupulosity in any tradition is an emotional matter, not a culturally determined phenomenon, usually relating back to one's position in the family of origin, but it is usually so disguised in cultural costume that it is often difficult to discern it from commitment.

In all events, if the myth of the shiksa and its cultural camouflage succeed in their deception, it becomes natural to assume that the families that would be most insistent on conversion would be those families that are most motivated by long-cherished traditional values. In some cases this is true, and in some it is not. A more consistent characterization of those families who make conversion into the dominant issue can be found in the following matrix, again phrased in terms of emotional process. The following seven characteristics of the way a family conceives of togetherness, and not any combination of cultural positions, are what I have found to be most true about those Jewish families that focus on conversion as a basis for acceptance.

1. The family is perceived to have a superself to which the self of each individual member is to be adapted emotionally.

2. Undifferentiated closeness is considered an automatic good, and acts of self that convey emotional autonomy are perceived to be "selfish."

3. The whole relationship system is conducive to panic because the circuit-breaker effect of self is missing. In fact, there is so much feedback in the anxiety circuits of such a family that it is almost impossible within such a relationship system to be objective about what is happening.

4. "Members of the tribe" who behave in ways that would take them out of the overall network of emotional interdependencies are perceived to be threatening. For where the whole family system is seen to be so dependent on each member, members of the family will feel they have to change also.

5. The greater family of the Jewish people is perceived in a similar, undifferentiated manner. Such a family tends, therefore, to overemphasize togetherness values in Judaism and to use the customs and traditions spawned by such values to keep its own personal family stuck together. The family members assume it is their Jewishness that is giving their family its kind of togetherness rather than the family that is putting Jewishness to its own neurotic service.

6. Any outsider to such a family is considered automatically threatening since that person has not been programmed to feel as the insiders. His or her very inclusion will change the system. The outsider does not have to be a non-Jew, but a non-Jew, because of the melding of feelings about family togetherness, is just that much more threatening.

7. Thinking in such families tends to go to extremes because of the totalistic quality of the emotional climate. A live-and-let-live approach is inconceivable. Solutions tend to be conceived in terms of pressuring the person not to change or to change back, nullifying the effects of the change by changing the outside agent of change (convert the non-Jew), cutting off the family member so the change will not change anyone else (sit *shiva*). To a large extent, non-Jews change in order to solve the Jewish partner's problems with his or her family.

There is a curious phenomenon about this stuck-togetherness thinking that actually can be used to the advantage of the bride and groom in stripping away the cultural camouflage. The rigidity of position of individuals who think about togetherness in an undifferentiated way makes it appear that they have great conviction about their beliefs. It is, however, not really their values or philosophical position that is paramount but rather their desire for emotional oneness. Thus, often when such relatives realize that there is no hope of swaying the child, it is they who convert, that is, become more accepting, in order to keep the family together, that is, "one."

Family Position and Marital Choice

The fourth aspect of the myth of the shiksa that has more to do with family process than cultural background is the essential question of who is most likely to intermarry. Most explanations have tended to go to one of two extremes: Jews who marry non-Jews are uncommitted, or, when they come from families that are strongly identified in their ethnicity, must be rebelling. Both of these explanations fail to grasp the relationship between family and culture being developed here, especially the role the emotional climate of a family plays in the original inculcation of values. Growing children are affected by their family's background, but I have found that the influence is not direct. The emotional climate of a family acts as a modulating force, screening, filtering, and coloring the background values and customs. Thus, the way any child in any family perceives and is influenced by the culture depends not on his or her position in the culture but on the position within the family.

I knew one mixed couple where the children were raised according to the culture of the same-sex parent. The Jewish father's son was sent to Hebrew school and the Gentile mother's daughter was sent to a Sunday school of her own religious background. Loving his mother, the boy grew up and married a Gentile woman. Loving her mother, the girl identified with her, and eventually married a Jewish man.

This emotional screening process exists in any family. It has more effect in strongly ethnic families. And it is especially present when the emotional system of the family, ethnic or not, is intense. It is, however, most influential for the focused child in an intense, ethnic family.

To clarify this relationship between ethnic identity and the family's own emotional climate, I will present two different examples involving two hypothetical Jewish families, the Cohens and the Levys. They are designed to illustrate how a family's cultural climate and the climate produced by that family's own emotional history shape the type of family position that tends to lead to mixed marriages.

The family history of the Cohens and Levys is identical; the degree of ethnic identification is not. In each family, the son was born within a year after the death of his paternal grandfather, replacing him in the feelings of the father. In each situation the original marriage was balanced by the mother's intense relationship with her own mother. Now let us posit that in each family when the maternal grandmother dies, her daughter — Mrs. Cohen or Mrs. Levy — puts the newly available emotional energy previously reserved for her mother into her son when she finds her husband unreceptive. In each family, then, the son would have become extremely important to each parent individually, as well as to the emotional balance of their marriage.

But let us say that one difference between the Cohens and Levys was that the Cohens were very Jewish, whether in a religious, ethnic, historical, or political way, but the Levys were not. Although the Levys were Jewish and in no way denied it, Judaism or Jewishness did not seem to occupy a very significant part of their thoughts or their activities. Then the odds favor the Cohens' son and not the Levys' son contracting a mixed marriage, even though the Cohens are actually "more Jewish."

But what if the Cohens and Levys have identical Jewish histories of deep cultural identification but different emotional histories?

This time the Levys have the same family emotional history as before, with the son triangled deeply into the emotional system of his parents. This is not so with the Cohens, however. For, unlike Mr. Levy, Mr. Cohen was not particularly significant to his own family: his nephew, not his son, was the grandchild who was born close in time to the death of his father. As for Mrs. Cohen, it is her sister rather than she who got stuck with the emotional responsibility for their mother. In this situation it would be the Levys, with the triangled and emotionally significant son, and not the Cohens who would be more likely to have their son marry a Gentile despite their strong cultural identification with Judaism.

This coincidence of family and ethnic background does not always create mixed marriage. Nor will it always be found in the background of every mixed marriage. It has shown up, however, more frequently than any set of sociological or cultural attributes and, as already mentioned, has created a theoretical framework for highly successful therapeutic intervention.

In a sense this fourth finding should have come first. It is, after all, more logical to begin with the family factors that influence who contracts mixed marriages and then go on to the emotional matrix that describes reacting relatives. I have purposely gone against that order because it is often only when we understand the reactions that we can understand their causes. So often they are part and parcel of the same process. In many situations the consequences are built in, so to speak. Certainly that is the way my own understanding of the entire phenomenon of Jewish-Gentile marriage unfolded. Only as I began to understand the depth of a parent's reaction to a son's marriage to a shiksa in terms of family history and family process did I then come to understand the depth and lure of her attraction.

The Universality of Cultural Camouflage

But the myth of the shiksa is not just a Jewish myth. First of all, families from almost any culture can be found that perceive outsiders as threats. All the same phenomena of hysteria, depression, and rejection can be found in other cross-cultural situations also. In fact, the most severe reaction I ever encountered in a parent was from a Greek Orthodox priest who threatened self-immolation if his daughter married out. And, if we carry things to their logical extreme, it should be pointed out that for a Mormon family in the holy citadel of Salt Lake City, the Jew is the Gentile.

Actually, the most famous shiksa in the twentieth century did not marry a Jew, but the king of England, who gave up his throne. As Queen Mary told Edward, her eldest son, his marriage to a divorced American was "destructive to his people, shameful to his family, a betrayal of his own upbringing." It was a relationship that would be "morally destructive." All this regal "Mrs. Portnoy" was missing was the culturally appropriate phrase. The true basis for the universality of the myth of the shiksa lies in the universality of the more general erroneous assumptions about family life that really give this Jewish myth so much power. Demythologizing the particular case leads to exposure of the universals.

Curiously, it is possible to use the in-group concept of the shiksa in reverse. Once it is recognized that the emotional phenomena described in the previous section are not particularly Jewish, then the constituent myths also lose their cover and the often hidden universal truths about family emotional process that those supporting myths mask also stand stripped of the disguise.

This section will be divided into two parts. First, I will show the universality of cultural camouflage as an emotional phenomenon. Next I will show how this hypothesis leads to the unveiling of other displacement myths that feed back and support the myth of the shiksa.

Cultural Camouflage, a Universal Phenomenon

Earlier I presented a list of statements made inadvertently in my office that showed a tendency of Jewish people to color the emotional processes of their family life Jewish. Here is a similar list of statements that I have collected in my office, this time made by individuals of various other cultural backgrounds.

- My husband has a typical Syrian temper.
- That's a typical Prussian way of distancing.
- In Japanese families the mother makes the wedding.
- If you're Catholic, you carry your cross till you die.
- German men are pushy.
- It's my English reserve — one doesn't wear dirty linen in public.
- My parents were Free Methodists — they never bought things on credit.
- The Irish don't bring up divorce at a wake.
- Europeans take things more seriously.
- In southern families the women are treated like slaves.
- It's my Anglo-Saxon background — peace at any price.
- Korean mothers don't teach their daughters about the kitchen.
- My father was a devout Baptist; that's why we never learned about sex.
- In Indian families bad things come in threes.
- I grew up with the inhibitions of the 1950s.
- It was a garden-variety close Huguenot family.
- Pakistani women have no sense of romance.
- I married an Italian; that should tell you something.
- Black women don't hate their mothers.

- In small Pennsylvania towns, you weren't allowed to talk back to your parents.

- I came from a typical European family where Father was the boss.

- In those days people didn't get divorced. [Australian]

- In those days people didn't get divorced. [Chinese]

- I grew up in a WASP family; you know — no affection.

- That's his Swiss mentality.

- Once you're baptized, your parents have got you.

- Episcopalians never tell secrets.

- Swedish families can't keep secrets.

- We always tried to date Jewish girls back at school, because everyone knows they're freer.

Clearly the emotional phenomenon by which the family process is disguised in cultural camouflage is universal. Below the surface it operates in two directions, often simultaneously. On the one hand, the family takes as distinctive to its own cultural background something that is really basic to the human condition, to family life in general. On the other hand, it takes something that is peculiar to its own idiosyncratic process and ascribes it more broadly to its cultural milieu. An example of both is contained in the term "Jewish mother" to describe a woman overly invested in her children, or as one Puerto Rican man described his "typical" Puerto Rican mother, "an energy source in search of an input." Obviously, not all Jewish mothers are "Jewish mothers," but then not all "Jewish mothers" are Jewish.

A more startling example, which also gives insight into the power of family process, is the Unitarian woman who said she was converting to Judaism because of "Unitarian guilt." Of all the "backgrounds" — we even hesitate to call it "cultural" because it is so young a tradition and so absent of specific customs — Unitarianism would seem to offer the least amount of cultural camouflage. This woman, however, was a fourth-generation Unitarian whose ancestors were among the New England founders of that church in the United States. For this woman, being a Unitarian really was a family affair.

But the very first time I began to question cultural cause and effect was after seeing a mixed couple where neither partner was Jewish. The wife had experienced three "breakdowns" during the course of her marriage to an engineer from Kentucky, whose mother was a Christian Science practitioner. She was a volatile woman from Mexico with a temperament that might be called "artistic." Her husband had married her because he did not like American women, who were always "so serious, so practical, and so concerned with getting things done." She had married him because she "did not like Mexican men, who showed such little respect for their wives," unlike American men, who "treated them with dignity." Eighteen years later, he had spent most of his marriage trying to figure out how he had chosen the one Mexican woman who was like all American women, and she was still trying to figure out how she had picked the one American man who was like all Mexican men.

Explaining away a family's emotional process is not the only way families avoid "owning up" to their own emotional heritage. The culture of the environment, the age, the physical conditions, even the sibling position are other popular forms of disguise. For example:

+ My father is cheap because he grew up during the Depression [despite the fact that his brother, Uncle Harry, can't hold on to a dime].

+ Aunt Rose is a prude because of the times in which she grew up [despite the fact that Aunt Mary, her kid sister, is a bunny].

+ I am frigid because I was raised with a very strict Catholic background [despite the fact that her sister keeps getting pregnant out of wedlock].

+ Why wouldn't you expect me to be adaptive in my marriage? The whole "culture" taught me to believe that women are the second sex [despite the fact that her sister, cousin, friend, and even her mother failed to get the message and are erroneously dominating their husbands].

Other familiar examples are:

+ I think my wife is insecure because her family moved about so much.

+ I can't communicate with my son because of the generation gap.

+ We should never have exposed him to all that violence on television.

+ She is going through the change of life.

- Our child was okay until he started associating with the wrong friends.

- He (I, she) was a middle (oldest, youngest, only) child.

Such explanations for family functioning tend to deny the family's responsibility for that functioning. It is just not evident, for example, that those whose ancestors came to the United States on the *Mayflower* will necessarily be more secure in marriage than those whose folks have just gotten off the boat. Cultural and environmental theories almost always fail to account for the fact that there are other families from the same background, or even other individuals from the same family, who are behaving differently.

It is true that sometimes there is the chance synchronization between a given family's style and certain outstanding attributes of that family's culture, so that the family is able to put aspects of the culture to its own neurotic service. When this occurs it is even more difficult to discern cause from effect. Authoritarian fathers who happen to be Mennonite or Catholic, possessive mothers who happen to be Jewish, prudish mothers who happen to be Methodist, adaptive women who happen to be Quaker — all will "hear" certain aspects of their tradition rather than others. Actually, what seems to occur is that all families of all cultures have a tendency to select or emphasize from their culture's repertoire of customs and ceremony those modes of behavior that fit their own style. And they most emphasize those values that tend to prevent change!

For example, I was once working with a Catholic family where the wife was the twin sister of a nun. When she went back home and started talking about the importance of self in marriage, her parents, secure in a mutually adaptive relationship in which they had both sacrificed their selves for togetherness, became anxious and told her to stop seeing a "Jewish" therapist since Christians believe in self-sacrifice. Whereupon the twin sister, whose specialty was theology, quoted a raft of Catholic theologians who had exalted the importance of self-respect and dignity.

If, however, we assume that it is the family emotional system rather than the ethnic or environmental background that does the real "culturing," then it is possible to develop an approach to the relationship of family and culture that keeps the responsibility where it belongs.

Displacement Myths and the Process of Change

Now I would like to present three examples of how cultural camouflage obscures the lines of responsibility in efforts to change a family. Each involves a widespread myth about family life that is reflected in the myth of the shiksa. But each, also, precisely because it is so widely believed, enhances the displacement and denial power of that particular myth in Jewish families. The areas of concern are compatibility in marriage, focus of discontent, and reasonableness and values as agents of change.

Compatibility. For the most part, families tend to think about marital compatibility in terms of similarity, and incompatibility in terms of difference. A great deal of emphasis in premarital counseling or matchmaking is placed on finding what individuals have in common. This is especially true when a mixed marriage is on the horizon, where couples are warned they already have "two strikes against them," but it tends to be true about all premarital ruminations even when the "kids" grew up on the "same side of the tracks." Similarly, when any match needs repairing, the couple will consider themselves as mismatched. That there is some difficulty with this notion is evident from the fact than when individuals with strikingly different sets of interests or backgrounds make it, the explanation usually given is "opposites attract."

The truth, of course, is that differences, whether cultural or of another kind, follow the same rules and play the same roles in all families. At times of stress, they become the focus of attention, and easily identifiable differences become the causes of the stress. But even when a difference becomes an issue, whether it is a difference in cultural background or a differing over anything else, that same difference does not cause problems every time it shows up. What determines whether background or other kinds of differences are repulsive or attractive are factors much more subtle than the so-called basic differences themselves. What seems to be crucial is not the ingredients of the mixture, but the overall emotional crucible into which it is poured. Incompatibility in marriage has less to do with the differences themselves than with what is causing them to stand out at that time.

The fact that families tend to ascribe their problems to their differences feeds back to the myth of the shiksa in two ways. First, it increases anxiety in the family and in the couple about their chances for marital success. Second, it does the exact opposite; it deludes the couple into thinking that the mates they have selected are far different (from their opposite-sex parent) than they really are.

A striking example of this phenomenon involved a highly educated, extremely well traveled and cultured Protestant woman from the Midwest who was marrying a Jewish English professor from New York. Her father, a bricklayer, was furious about the marriage. During the courtship, her mother, who was also opposed, developed cancer and died within a few months. Father (an extremely passive man in his marriage who let Mother take all the responsibility and kept her adaptive to him with constant putdowns) then began to blame his daughter for her mother's death. As the daughter changed in response to the way she handled both her mother's death and her father's reactions, her fiancé made more and more noises about how she had changed, how rigid and cold she had become, and how he could not "get through" to her anymore.

He began to complain that she did not understand his dilemma as a Jew marrying a woman whose father was anti-Semitic. Next he spoke about his fears that with this new pattern of "withdrawal" she might abandon him emotionally in their marriage. He blamed it all on the fact that she was "denying" her mother's death.

Another type of cultural "fake-out" is the situation where, after a period of extreme mutual hostility, Jewish mother and shiksa daughter-in-law gravitate towards one another, drawn by the similarity with which they generally relate, namely, laser-beam focus on another person. In this process, which I have dubbed the *crossover,* the triangle shifts, and instead of Jewish husband and non-Jewish wife being in alliance against Jewish mother, it is now Jewish husband who is the outsider as the two women exchange recipes from their respective backgrounds. I have seen this occur with African American, Pakistani, Chinese, and Appalachian shiksas.

Focus of Discontent. It is not only stressful issues that family members are prone to consider as causes rather than symptoms; other members of the family are also often perceived to be a source of anxiety when they are really the focus of the anxiety. Husbands and wives often displace their own existential discontent on their spouse, their discontent with one another on a child, their discontent with a parent on an in-law, and so forth. And it is obviously crucial for effective therapy, as well as long-lasting change, that both the therapist and the family be able eventually to distinguish a cause of discontent from a focus of discontent.

Failure to make this distinction preserves the focus as a displacement, for, as with the culture-family process syndrome, the content (in this case, the information presented about the focused person) is seen as causative rather than illustrative of the reporter's anxiety. That is exactly what the myth of the shiksa is all about. Not only is the shiksa no longer a non-Jewish woman; today she is not even a woman — that is, a person. The shiksa today is a focus of discontent, and as I have tried to show, she tends to rise with all her own mythology to the imagination of certain Jewish families not because she is non-Jewish, but rather because that Jewish family at that particular moment does not wish to take responsibility for the way it is put together.

Once again, however, the more general myth is not only reflected in the myth of the shiksa, but supports it. For the widespread fashion in which families equate the focus of their discontent with the cause of their misery makes it all the more difficult for a couple to understand why they have "triggered" so much hostility or why they have been so unsuccessful in their reasonable efforts to calm the family down. As can be the case with even the most experienced therapist, what the couple has unwittingly done is to accept that focus by their very efforts to change the family's views. Despite their good intentions, because those efforts were directed at the content of the issues, they became part of the family's process of denial.

Of course, the fact that with the shiksa the displaced focus is on cultural difference adds to the identifying process and creates a doubly reinforced displacement. But all forms of denial are in secret allegiance.

Reasonableness and Values as Agents of Change. In my training and supervising of family therapists, whether they be clergy, social workers, psychologists, nurses, or psychiatrists; whether they live in the East or the West, the United States or Europe; whether they work for organizations or privately; and regardless of their social, religious, or cultural backgrounds, I have been struck by one extraordinarily similar aspect of their thinking — their reliance on reasonableness and values as instruments of change. I believe this is part and parcel of the "content thinking" that is the hallmark of cultural emphases.

The kind of experience with mixed marriage that I have been describing, in which emotional process almost always overrides cultural values, raises suspicions about the efficacy of such reliance on reason.

It is only logical to assume that members of a family, blessed with a cortex and the power of speech, can be changed by resorting to these inherent tools. However, my experience with trying to bring change to families reacting to a mixed marriage suggests that families who are in distress tend to "think with their spinal cords" rather than their cortex, and when thought processes are of that kind, the values expressed are not so much evidence of what motivates family members as symptoms of emotional positions they have already arrived at.

In this essay on the relationship between culture and family process in the formation of Jewish identity, I tried to explain the failure of the emphasis on cultural content to produce a stronger identity. I suggested that such content could be compared to the fuel needed to run a motor, but that we could not make a vehicle go forward by simply filling it with gas if the "transmission" was in neutral, let alone reverse. When the emotional system is ignored and the focus remains on cultural content, communication has the effect of typing a message on a word processor when the power has been turned off. When it comes to changing families, since all families are supplied by their culture with an infinite variety of rationalizations for their behavior, a focus on values and ideological positions is often just another form of displacement. To offer reasonable alternatives to such positions, therefore, is once again only to *conspire* in the family's denial of its emotional process.

It has been my experience in working with families of all backgrounds that rather than values or reason, power is the most forceful agent of change. This is not the power of conquest and domination but rather the strength to get enough distance from the anxiety maelstrom whirling around us to think out our own values, whether or not they coincide with values from our own background, to define them clearly, and then to have the strength to hold that position against the efforts of others to change us back. In other words, the most powerful agent of change comes more out of a focus on our own values than on trying to define the values of others.

Therefore the widespread but erroneous belief that expressed values are the cause of family members' positions and that, therefore, change in a given family member's functioning can be brought about by appealing to or changing those values, simply escalates anxiety and resistance on both sides. For it encourages a process wherein each side is perpetually trying to define, convince, change, and, therefore, *convert* the other.

Summary

In summary, I have endeavored to demythologize the myth of the shiksa in Jewish families and at the same time to show how that particular myth provides a laboratory for observing the way other widespread myths of family life prevent change in families everywhere. The broader myths all have some relationship to one generally misunderstood notion about the relationship of culture and family process. Once that relationship is understood to be almost the reverse of what is often assumed, new perceptions become available for understanding all families, as well as for creating strategies for therapeutic change.

Five

METAPHORS OF SALVATION

There is an emerging intellectual and professional ferment now bubbling in family therapy circles throughout the country. This ferment carries special significance here in the Washington area, where the originators and major representatives of several of the best-known schools of family therapy reside and conduct their training. While such diversity may produce added confusion for local practitioners and students, it also carries the potential of creating more exciting opportunities for challenge and growth.

I would like to take a historical perspective in viewing the current rivalries among the various belief systems that comprise the field of family therapy. First, as someone who has been intimately involved over the past quarter-century in the theory and practice of three different systems of salvation — politics, religion, and psychotherapy — I will recall some personal experiences that may shed some light on some characteristic responses that occur when those outside the "faith" challenge one's belief system. Second, I will describe some uncanny parallels in the issues various systems of salvation encounter in their efforts to bring about change. Third, I would like to present some of my own conclusions about the perennial human search for salvation that have proved helpful to me in trying to sort out and sometimes mix the metaphors of family therapy.

The Psychotherapeutic Reformation

Today family therapy is one of almost a hundred therapeutic modalities. It was not always so. I can remember a time when, at least here in

First published as "Mixing the Metaphors of Salvation" in *Family Therapy Network Newsletter* 5, no. 2 (March–April 1981): 1–3.

the Washington area, psychotherapy was practically synonymous with psychoanalysis. There were other therapeutic schools, and they had their practitioners, but the *Magna Carta* of the nonmedical therapist (the system of third-party payments) was not promulgated until the 1960s. Two incidents from this period may show how far things have come since then.

Back in the 1950s, several ministers who had read everything Freud had written, who had undergone psychoanalysis themselves, and who ascribed to the lay analysis model of Theodor Reik formed an association of pastoral counselors and began to see patients several times a week. Some members of the local psychoanalytic society became furious, as they claimed, "out of concern for the local patient population." Their fury abated only when the pastoral counselors agreed to see all their patients *sitting up*. Then, several years later, there was the rabbi who sent out a brochure about his efforts to create a referral service in which he innocently used the term "diagnosis." For this indiscretion he was reported to the State Board of Medicine for "practicing medicine without a license." He was allowed to continue unharassed only if he stopped using "that word" despite the fact that part of his defense was, "Every Sears store in town also has a diagnostic center." Such things would be unthinkable today.

In the concern with rite (lying on the couch) and the tremendous connotative power of certain sacred words ("diagnosis"), these incidents carry echoes of historic debates that have taken place within other systems of salvation. It is my perception that since World War II, psychotherapy has gone through an intellectual and technical upheaval rivaling in intensity and import the struggle for humankind's soul that occurred during the Protestant Reformation five hundred years ago. The aftermath of this contemporary reformation has been a myriad of sects arguing about rites and sacred words. Today, instead of clashing over issues of faith vs. works, we argue about the role of insight vs. behavior change. Each new therapeutic denomination ambivalently attacks and borrows from the mother church (psychoanalysis) as it defines its own identity. Each has its own view of man, sin, and atonement. Each has its own holy works, priesthoods, saints, sacred societies, and heretics. (Actually, everyone sees everyone else as a heretic.) Some emphasize dependency on the spiritual leader. Some say "every man is his own priest." Some emphasize rite or method, others awakening. Some seem like small cults, such as the followers of Henry Stack Sullivan. Some (the Esalen Institute) are more charismatic, while others (primal scream therapy) are tinged with apocalypse. Today disciples, not to mention apostles, proliferate, often hearing the same master differently.

Some Intriguing Parallels

During my early days in Washington, I had an experience that brought home to me psychotherapy's parallels with both religion and politics. The local psychoanalytic society had invited seven clergy of different faiths, including myself, to meet regularly with seven society members for a year. During those meetings it seemed that we discussed every conceivable notion about the nature of human existence and the difficulty of bringing about change. As I sat in these discussions, I began to realize that at no time did the division of opinions ever break along professional or religious lines. No matter what the issue, the group never lined up with clergy vs. the analysts, or the clergy and the analysts of one faith vs. those of another. Then it occurred to me that I had observed a similar process during my experiences in the political arena. In the early 1960s, before the passage of fair housing legislation, I had worked as a community relations specialist for the White House, flying into different urban areas to help citizen committees integrate local housing facilities. I found that sociological and professional differences among committee members rarely accounted for their differences of opinion. When it came to drawing up integration timetables, deciding how to start and how aggressive to be, whether to emphasize direct action or education, there was no way to predict where a person would stand just from his color or his professional status.

It eventually dawned on me that every salvation system, either implicitly or explicitly, must come to terms with a certain set of core issues. Politics, religion, and psychotherapy all have their different metaphors for conceptualizing the human dilemma. They each blame different devils. But when one considers their various methods for freeing human beings from what enslaves or possesses them (their conceivable "rites of exorcism"), there is almost no difference at all. Each of the issues common to all salvation systems may be represented as a continuum along which a spectrum of opinion is possible. These core issues include point of attack (some talk about the symptom, others the system); how to motivate (some emphasize thought, others feeling); style of leadership (some seek charisma, others want consensus); achieving lasting change (some say through insight, others say through behavior); flexibility regarding one's beliefs (some are purists, some eclectic). Those issues may be said to define our capacity to view the human condition and conceive of new ways to bring about change. Focusing on these as the underlying constructs that guide our thinking enables us to understand how often our intellectual "sophistication" turns out to be illusory. Many people today no longer believe in the supernatural but accept with perfect faith the prime-mover quality of the subconscious. In switching from "super" to "sub," have these people changed anything but their metaphor or their pew?

Some Guidelines for Self-Salvation

What then of the metaphors of family therapy and present efforts to compare, contrast, and perhaps integrate them? Is it all relative, merely a matter of the "church" to which one belongs or the "service" one regularly attends (Haley's "Methodism," Bowen's "Fundamentalism," or Minuchin's "Sacraments")? Is there any real merit in the search for some organized way of viewing the field?

I believe there is, provided it can avoid the extremes of pell-mell ecumenism on the one hand or dogmatic proselytizing on the other. The dangers of an overly hasty ecumenism may be illustrated by the following tale.

In the midst of a recent conversation, Jay Haley asked me, "What's the difference between a Bowen reversal and my paradoxical approach?" I responded, much too quickly, "When Bowen does a reversal he is primarily concerned with himself, with getting out of the feedback position. But the purpose of the paradox is to directly affect the head of the patient." Jay then responded, "That's funny. I always thought I was presenting paradox to get out of the position of helper." So Bowen and Haley are really the same! But with that logic one can, upon hearing a Hasidic melody in the midst of Beethoven's *Eroica* (it's in the third movement),

prove that Beethoven was a Hasid. As most musicologists would con-
tend, to truly appreciate the difference between musical systems one must
focus on the mode (the creative matrix), not the melody.

The dangers of proselytizing as a way of validating one's own beliefs
are more subtle. These dangers can be reduced, however, if one keeps
in mind that the search for ways of better defining one's own system of
meaning is its own greatest reward. "Good" questions are more important than "right" answers. The kinds of questions we ask determine the
range of answers we can conceive. My experience with the metaphors
of religion, politics, and psychotherapy has led me to four guidelines for
keeping my own head on straight.

Models

The purpose of a theoretical model (e.g., the Freudian psyche of id, ego,
and super-ego) is to give meaning to perceptions and make experience
coherent. Long-term use of a particular model, however, makes it easy
to confuse metaphor with reality. The best clue I have found that one
has taken one's model too seriously is when one can no longer appreciate or understand the metaphors of others except when they have been
rephrased into one's own terms ("What you're really saying is … ").

The Mission of the Priesthood

Every salvation system has its group of leaders, its "priesthood," who
communicate the values of that system to those who seek to be "saved."
The mission of this priesthood may be represented along a dependency
continuum stretching from prescribing simple remedies and totally re-
lieving pain at one extreme to helping others develop their own solutions
and increasing their capacity to tolerate and cope with pain at the
other. Moving towards eliminating pain usually focuses one on comfort
and "answers." Erring in the direction of tolerance for discomfort and
ambiguity is more likely to keep the focus on challenge and questions.

Nonbelievers

Here the guideline is, can one relate to those of a different "faith" without needing to convert them? In politics this position would be illustrated
by the following definition: "The true liberal is one who can have a meaningful relationship with an arch-conservative." The danger to avoid is

developing a belief system that identifies others as damned or lost, which then puts us in the position of having to save them rather than being able to learn from them.

Application

The final guideline flows from and subsumes the first three. It is important to differentiate between applying one's system directly to others or primarily to oneself. In the latter case, it is the personhood of the believer rather than the principles of his belief system that becomes the beneficial factor in the lives of others. There was an old Hasidic master who once said, "The world would be far better off if, instead of being concerned about our own bodies and other people's souls, we watched over other people's bodies and our own souls." Such a position implies a philosophy of transference that minimizes projection and maximizes search.

Those four guidelines are in no way meant to be foolproof or all-inclusive, and they are certainly not easy to abide by. They are simply the conclusions of one family therapist who, after watching the great debates in religion, politics, and psychotherapy, has wound up with a tendency to be doctrinaire in theory and eclectic in practice.

Six

THE PLAY'S THE THING

The Therapeutic Reversal as Psychodrama

PROLOGUE

DATE: 1953

LOCATION: A rehearsal of Sheridan's *School for Scandal* at the Bucknell
                  University Theater

DIRECTOR: Ed, there's a way of delivering a line so that the audience
                  knows that you know what they know.

DATE: 1968

LOCATION: Supervisory session in the office of Dr. Murray Bowen

SUPERVISOR: Ed, there's a way of saying these things so that the person
                  is affected by what you say even though that person knows
                  what you are doing.

The history of theater is filled with examples of dramatists communicating a full grasp of complex human technical shorthand that we therapists so often use. When Hamlet, for example, responds to Ophelia's indignant rebuffs of his advances with the famous line, "Methinks the lady

Originally presented at Georgetown University Medical School, March 20, 1980, as "The
Therapeutic Reversal as Psychodrama." First published in *The Family Therapy Networker* 8,
no. 1 (January–February 1984): 2–9.

doth protest too much," we can be sure that Shakespeare's understanding of reaction formation did not come from his weekly sessions with his analyst.

When Othello, crazed with jealousy, accuses Desdemona of betraying him, and at the same time directs her how to respond to his accusations, we know he did not get his understanding of double binds from the Stratford-on-Avon Family Institute. Similarly, any family therapist on first reading August Strindberg's nineteenth-century play *The Dance of Death* will be amazed by the author's insight into the destructive potential of emotional triangles. And a magnificent training tape on the problems of remaining objective in intense relationship systems is the great Japanese film *Rashoman*.

But if it is possible to wonder at the psychological insight of gifted dramatists, it is equally possible to be astounded by the dramatic gifts of effective therapists. After years of observing Jay Haley, Murray Bowen, Norman Paul, Carl Whitaker, and others, I have begun to wonder if they would not have made great playwrights. At times I have even thought maybe that's what they really are. After all, to go back to *Othello*, what's wrong with the notion that double binding, either the pathogenic or the therapeutic variety, is generated by stage directions from a director acting in his own play?

Clearly a case could be made that both dramatists and therapists use some of the same techniques — paradox, staging, sides, scripting, creating catharsis. The similarity, however, goes deeper than the use of a related set of techniques. Both theater and therapy share a common impulse — an attempt to go beyond the everyday forms of communication to shift people's basic notions of themselves and their world. Both represent a revolt against the normal use of discourse, an understanding of the natural limits of rhetoric, and a recognition that communication is at least as much an emotional phenomenon as a linguistic one. They have borrowed from one another over the years, but much that is similar is due not to such mutual exchange but rather to their common cause. (Even the divisions of opinion that polarize their communities are identical.)

Soon I began to realize that it was impossible to isolate the "technique" of paradox — whether in theater or therapy — from the paradox of life. Similarly, I began to realize that absurdity in theater and therapy was an inevitable response to the absurdity of existence.

Still, I was not sure how best to describe the connections I had found. Finally I decided to borrow from the very discipline in which I was immersing myself. What follows is a series of "scenes," brief vignettes that on one level are excursions into the history of drama but that also, as will become clear by the epilogue, are comments on our daily performances in the theater of therapy.

Scene I / Oedipus, Everyman, and the Betamax

Words communicate, words persuade; words inspire the imagination. But why, for all their power, are words so powerless in eliciting fundamental change? Why has all the splendid oratory of the great political reformers and social visionaries not moved people more? Why, to bring the question closer to home, do all the well-reasoned words we utter in therapy, founded in solid theory and delivered to clients eagerly seeking change, not have more impact?

Most of the world's religions, for all their emphasis on holy writ and the sacred teachings of the masters, have understood the limitations of words. From the very beginning it was realized that even holy words were not necessarily efficacious. In fact, drama first emerged out of a desire to add spectacle and intensity to religious observance. The first medicine men were thespians, and the evolution from hocus-pocus to ritual to theater was a natural effort to go beyond the everyday use of words. It is one thing to deliver a sermon to a congregation informing them that death is the great equalizer and cannot be escaped; it is quite another to put Death, Good Deeds, Friendship, and Everyman in an allegory upon a stage and have them talk to one another. This is what happens in the medieval play *Everyman*, a theatrical event widely considered a landmark in the Western dramatic tradition. *Everyman* originated as an attempt to go beyond just "pointing out the problem" with words.

As with the medieval morality plays, the tragedies and comedies of the Greeks were originally created for religious festivals. Anyone who has been up into the mountains beyond Athens and stood in the great amphitheater of Epidauras cannot help but feel awed at its setting. There are no confines to that theater; the sky is the ceiling, the hills are the walls against that ceiling. Tradition has it that the cries of Oedipus and Agamemnon still echo in a perpetual ricochet between those walls. Anyone first hearing the words of Sophocles, Euripides, or Aeschylus in that vast playhouse had to have heard more than was actually spoken. Surely, viewing the sorrows and the sins of Clytemnestra, the pity of Iphigenia, the multigenerational legacy of Orestes must have brought more awareness of the conflicts of fate and individuality than the more prosaic Delphic Oracles could produce.

Today, of course, we can hear and view our own "performance," for we have the tape recorder and TV. But can these improvements really help us see ourselves and our conflicts mirrored on the "stage"? For over the years, I have continually noted that those clients who record their sessions seem to have a hidden mental switch which always has the uncanny ability with Watergate efficiency to erase the most significant passages. And I will never forget the marvelous time that I observed split-screen technique employed to record people watching their own recording. For, as their body "language" while observing was identical to their movements on the screen, it brought about great awareness for me, the audience. I doubt it did much for those in the "play." Now one could have split the screen again, and viewed them viewing themselves. But change, by its nature, is hardly an infinite regression.

Scene II / Stanislavsky vs. Brecht: Aesthetic Distance

As therapists we often puzzle over the role of distance in human relationships: how to separate people who are too involved, how to bring together people who are too separate. Although too much emotional or physical distance can inhibit communication, understanding, and love, too much closeness can limit objectivity and awareness. Each day we make decisions about whether new perceptions are best fostered in an atmosphere of intellectual detachment or one of emotional intensity.

Today, our field is divided about the role that psychological distance plays in helping people to change. Should a family therapist try to maintain a neutral interpretive stance, minimize transference, and encourage family members to be more objective? Or should therapists use their full expressive range to create a provocative therapeutic environment?

A look at the history of drama shows we are not alone in our concern with the problem of distance. Just as some maximize and some minimize the transference in therapy, playwrights and directors have long argued about whether the audience's empathy and emotional proximity to the characters on stage should be lessened or increased. At one extreme is Konstantin Stanislavsky, the late-nineteenth-century director of the Moscow Art Theater and the originator of "method-acting." Stanislavsky believed that if actors totally eliminated the distance between themselves and their parts, they would promote a similar feeling of closeness between the audience and their character.

In contrast to Stanislavsky, the German playwright Bertholt Brecht dedicated himself to limiting the audience's empathy and identification with the actors on stage. Brecht was more interested in creating what he called "aesthetic distance." In plays like *The Caucasian Chalk Circle* and *The Good Woman of Setzuan*, Brecht is careful to develop his plot and characters only to the point at which he decides that the audience might be too caught up in the illusion on stage to evaluate it thoughtfully. At such moments Brecht typically creates something to distance the audience: an actor might sing a song or read a poem that is "out of character." Brecht called this an "alienation effect" (A-effect), a distancing mechanism designed to provide the audience with an aesthetic perspective promoting greater awareness of the complex drama unfolding before them.

Brecht's description of the alienation effect hints at the family therapy camp in which he might feel most comfortable today:

> The first condition for the A-effect application is that stage and auditorium must be purged of everything "magical" and that no "hypnotic" tensions should beset us...no attempt is made to put [the audience] in a trance.... The audience's tendency to plunge into such illusions has to be checked constantly.
>
> The A-effect [enhances] the freedom of the actor's relationship with his audience in that he does not treat it as an *undifferentiated mass* [italics mine].... The rejection of empathy is not the action of emotions, nor does it lead to such. The crude aesthetic thesis that emotions can only be stimulated by means of empathy is wrong.... There are many contemporary works of art where one

can speak of the decline in emotional effectiveness due to their isolation from reason or the revival of emotion thanks to a stronger rationalist message.

Taking a position somewhere between Stanislavsky and Brecht is Edward Boulough, whose 1911 essay "Psychical Distance," written a decade before Freud wrote on the same subject, contains a complete analysis of the problems of transference (although this was not the term Boulough used). Boulough describes how both actors and audiences can be "underdistanced" or "overdistanced." The underdistanced person jumps up on the stage and saves the heroine from the villain. Today, it is the sports fan who throws a squash at the referee or the mother who interferes in her daughter's wedding by taking over all the arrangements. The overdistanced person, on the other hand, is totally unable to appreciate what he perceives because "They didn't do it right" or "The play should have been written another way." He is personally uninvolved. Boulough concludes that the ideal viewer relationship is to minimize distance without losing it altogether.

Reading Stanislavsky, Brecht, and Boulough on the problems of "aesthetic distance," one may well wonder whether Freud's understanding of the transference/countertransference phenomenon has its roots in his knowledge of theater. Despite all his efforts to establish psychoanalysis as the science of the human mind, Freud came out four-square against medical training for analysts. In *The Question of Lay Analysis,* his defense of nonphysician Theodor Reik's right to practice psychoanalysis, Freud strongly recommends that the analyst's background should be in the humanities, especially history and the arts. The Greek word *aesthetein* means "perception."

Scene III / The Seriousness of Tragedy and the Tragedy of Seriousness

In the history of theater, satire does not flourish in romantic periods. Shakespeare aside, the same dramatist might write both comedies and tragedies, but rarely both sonnets and parodies. The seriousness of love does not encourage appreciation of the ludicrous, but neither does the seriousness of psychosis. It is perhaps not accidental that we use the word "committed" to mean both an attribute of steadfastness leading to monogamy as well as the state of being confined to a mental institution. What is it about love that destroys perspective or about perspective that destroys love? What is it about seriousness that can lead to romance or invention on the one hand, murder and schizophrenia on the other? What is it about seriousness that can lead to the creation of beauty or obscure reality, that can galvanize energy or immobilize initiative? Growth, art, all accomplishments require that life be taken seriously. One of the great tragedies of life is the proportion of humanity who fail in this realization. And yet, taken too seriously, life can lose meaning. Is it simply a matter of proportion, a time to laugh and a time to cry?

The most serious romance I know is John Synge's *Deirdre of the Sorrows*. Synge, better known for *The Playboy of the Western World,* had a way with words rivaled in the English language perhaps only by Dylan Thomas. "In a good play," he wrote in 1907, "every speech should be flavored as a nut or apple.... In Ireland, for a few years more we have a popular imagination that is fiery and magnificently tender, so that those of us who wish to write start with a chance that is not given to writers in places where the springtime of the local life has been forgotten, and the harvest is memory only, and straw has been turned into bricks."

In *Deirdre,* an old king finds a beautiful little girl and raises her for the day she will become his queen. But before this can happen she runs off with a man she meets one day in the woods. They spend seven years on some small islands in the Irish Sea. After the seventh year, the king sends a messenger of peace to bring them back. The couple knows it is a trick, but still they return. Why? Because they have had such an idyllic romance that they have begun to fear that with age they will tire of one another and they don't want their perfect love to ever spoil. So they return, Deirdre's lover is killed by the king, and Deirdre decides, against all advice, to join him in the grave.

It is impossible to capture the beauty of Synge's language, the power of the play, by simply re-telling it. Deirdre's fate, like the fate of many great fictional characters, can be explained as the result of excessive romantic seriousness. There are, of course, other "serious" ways of looking at Deirdre's dilemma. One might reduce Deirdre's decision to kill herself to a consequence of her being part of an "enmeshed system." A "serious" family therapist watching the play might want to consult with Deirdre before she makes her fateful decision and tell her, "Deirdre, you must get out of the fusion. You need another relationship system. Deirdre, the intensity of your love was due to the fact that you have no extended family. Your talk about being unable to go on alone is a 'no-self' attitude towards life. You must get some distance."

Perhaps Deirdre's downfall had to do with how seriously she took love and life. But the seriousness of such clinical remarks, reducing existential complexities to textbook pathology, have the character of psychosis. On the other hand, we have all experienced people who are so serious about their existence that to take them seriously is crazy.

How then shall we distinguish between the seriousness of tragedy and the tragedy of seriousness? Here is a suggestion. The most serious play I know is not really *Deirdre* or *Agamemnon, Oedipus* or *Lear,* or even Ibsen's *Ghosts,* in which the author omits a conventional denouement and thus leaves the audience no way out. It is rather O'Neill's *Long Day's Journey into Night.*

One day, a young woman came to my office and offered a soul-wrenching account of her life. She sounded as if she was an original member of the Tyrone family in *Long Day's Journey into Night,* a play which packs more family pathology into two hours than any drama I've ever seen. As she spoke of her alcoholic father, her less-than-innocent mother, the rows among her siblings, I kept thinking of O'Neill's play. Finally I asked, "Are you familiar with *Long Day's Journey into Night?*" "Familiar with it?" she responded. "It was the story of my life. I used to read it regularly, discussed it on all my dates, even wrote college themes about it." But she, alas, had learned little from the travails of the Tyrones that might enable her to shift the direction of her own life.

She approached reading about the tragedy of the Tyrones with the same seriousness she approached all her problems. What never occurred to her was that the seriousness with which she confronted life might have been more the cause of her difficulties than their effect.

Seriousness presents a paradox. If family members are not serious about their responsibilities, the family may become unstable and chaotic. But seriousness can also be destructive. This side of seriousness is more than an attitude; it is a total orientation, a way of thinking embedded in constant, chronic anxiety. It is characterized by lack of flexibility in response, a narrow repertoire of approaches, persistent efforts to try harder, an inability to change direction, and loss of perspective.

Such serious families surround themselves with volatile fumes of anxiety; any small incident can create a flare-up. They will always assume that it was the incident that created the problem, but it is the way they relate and think that gives any incident its inflammatory power. The family caught in its ongoing drama tends to confuse the focus of its discontent with the cause of its misery.

So often in therapy we attempt to alter the course of a family's drama. Typically, however, the more serious the family is about the drama, the harder it is to introduce the possibility of change. It is in an atmosphere of play, rather than intense seriousness, that such shifts are likely to take place.

It was a formerly child-focused mother who first brought this home to me. I had just mentioned a recent article that maintained that care for the young and the capacity to be playful both emerge at the same stage in the development of the mammalian brain. "Oh, yes," the woman responded in an isn't-that-obvious sort of way. "I used to worry all the time about how much attention to give my children, fearful that I wasn't giving them enough, anxious that I was overinvolved. But since I've discovered how to be more playful, I find keeping the right distance just isn't a problem."

How then shall we distinguish between the seriousness of tragedy and the tragedy of seriousness? Here is what I learned from these two clients: When the seriousness is in the *plot,* we are dealing with the seriousness of tragedy, but when the seriousness is in the *character,* we are dealing with a tragic flaw. In therapy there can be no hope for preventing that latter type of tragedy till the seriousness has been relocated in the plot.

Scene IV / Who the Devil's the Devil? The Authentic Shaw

Several years ago at a dinner party I suddenly found myself caught defending the reputation of a mentor of mine well-known for saying things he really didn't believe. Assailed by accusations that such "reversers" were not authentic, I finally saw an escape. "Look," I said, "what you all don't seem to grasp is that Murray Bowen is a devil. So when he does all those devilish things, for him it's really authentic." Exasperated, furious, and very serious, the opposition cried out, "You just did one!" The rest of the evening went well.

I have always thought that the word "authenticity" should be reserved for rare stamps and books. To apply the concept of authenticity to human beings seems authoritarian. The Spanish Inquisitors would have loved the concept for, from an unquestioning belief in the truth of authenticity, it is but a short step to a nonacceptance of differences and a tyranny of goodness that restricts the act of becoming. In family therapy, the steadfast concern with authenticity can rob both therapist and motivated family members of one of their most effective initiatives — their capacity to be mischievous.

Over the past seventeen years I have perhaps on a dozen occasions conducted sessions in which nothing I said was "from the heart." Every response was ludicrous, crazy, even silly. So mad was it that someone overhearing the conversation in my office could easily have thought I was the patient. But every one of those episodes turned out to be one of the most fruitful I have ever experienced. Each time I was "prompted" to "act" this way by a sense of hopeless stuckness with the family, and each time I got into the role, it was as though I were personifying the neurotic unconscious of family members, saying the very words that when they said them to themselves prevented change. Each time, once I had "become the part," I found myself able to think their thoughts better than they, and in the process obtain more insight into their thinking than had I tried to interpret theirs. And each time I became their "alter-subconscious" rather than their "alter-ego," they wound up far removed from the rigidity of perception with which they entered. Yet throughout, they were never sure whether any of my responses was serious (nor was I).

It can even be used in didactic lectures. For example, getting up before a PTA as an expert on children and speaking on: "How to Get Your Kid to Drop Out and Save 50,000 Dollars in Tuition."

It is absolutely clear to me where I learned to be such a devil. Not from Haley or Bowen or Milan, but from George Bernard Shaw, whose munitions' manufacturer shows incredible benevolence for his workers (*Major Barbara*), and whose devil (*Don Juan in Hell*) is a delightful intellect.

I still remember vividly how my head became totally twisted around as I heard Don Juan and the devil speak totally out of character, and I realized from that moment on the extraordinary impact of having the wrong person say the right thing but always costumed in a twinkle. ("Oldests" have much less capacity to do this than "youngests" or "onlys" and may skip immediately to the next scene.)

In all his plays Shaw questions the authentic but perhaps none more than in the Don Juan sequence from *Man and Superman*. Don Juan the philanderer turns out to be a philosopher; his archenemy, Doña Ana's father, his friend; and together with Doña Ana, who is the epitome of authentic virtue, all end up in hell. Indeed, the latter's surprise foreshadows *The Devil in Ms. Jones* as she wonders aloud, "And I could have been so much more wickeder."

But why the mirror image of the Don Juan legend? Why has left become right, and right, wrong? To set the stage for the more profound reversals of perception to come on all the truths we hold so dear:

The Devil (really Shaw) on women:

> But how rash and dangerous it was for woman to invent a separate creature whose sole function was her own impregnation! For mark what has happened. She has been unable to employ for her purposes more than a fraction of the immense energy she has left at his disposal by saving him the exhausting labor of gestation. This superfluous energy has gone to his brain and to his muscle. He has become too strong to be controlled by her bodily, and too imaginative...to be content with mere self-reproduction. He has created civilization without consulting her, taking her domestic labor for granted as the foundation of it.

The Devil (really Shaw) on virtue:

> In the arts of peace man is a bungler. His heart is in his weapons. This marvellous force of life of which you boast is a force of Death: Man measures his strength by his destructiveness. The plague, the famine, the earthquake, the tempest were too spasmodic in their action; the tiger, the crocodile were too easily satiated and not cruel enough. Something more constantly, more ruthlessly, more ingeniously destructive was needed, and that something was Man, the inventor of

the rack, the stake, the gallows, the electrocutor; of the sword and gun; above all of justice, duty, patriotism, and all the other -isms by which even those who are clever enough to be humanely disposed are persuaded to become the most destructive of destroyers.

Don Juan (really Shaw) on devils:

In this palace of lies a truth or two will not hurt you. Your friends are but beautiful: they are only decorated. They are not dignified: they are only fashionably dressed. They are not religious: they are only pew-renters. They are not prosperous; they are only rich; not public spirited, only patriotic; not determined, only obstinate; not intelligent, only opinionated; not just, only vindictive; and not truthful at all — liars every one of them to the very backbone of their souls.

Friedman on authenticity:

SCENE: The 8th Day of Creation

HOLY ONE: Satan, I need a curse, one that will last forever. It must be so much a part of man's nature that his capacity to be tenacious will perpetuate it.

SATAN: I got one, boss. No one will marry the person who's good for them. Everyone will choose someone who brings out their weaknesses and we'll mask it all in a fog called romance.

HOLY ONE: Sounds terrific. But suppose some of these new creatures grow because of this experience and become like one of us?

SATAN: We'll create an institution called divorce; then they can be free to make the same mistakes while thinking they made a change.

HOLY ONE: Not good enough. These creatures are very smart; some might even rise above that.

SATAN: I think I know what to do, and the great thing is it will also use man's persistence against himself.

HOLY ONE: Wonderful, what's it going to be called?

SATAN: How about family therapy?

Scene V / Characters in Search of an Author: Pirandello on Paradox

All disciplines sooner or later develop conventions which then define what is unconventional. Sometimes, however, novelty is introduced in a way that is more than nonconventional. The new idea or approach does not fit the established dichotomies of convention and yet seizes the imagination in a way that prevents it from just being rejected. When this happens, we have what Kuhn called a "paradigm shift." Such a shift occurred in twentieth-century theater when Luigi Pirandello wrote a trilogy of plays that turned theater inside out. The most famous of these, *Six Characters in Search of an Author,* drew a response something like a family therapy research project being reviewed by a 1950s NIMH panel of psychoanalysts. It wasn't that the critics disagreed or rejected it; they simply hadn't the foggiest what it was about.

In *Six Characters,* five people (the sixth comes on later) invade a re-hearsal of another Pirandello play. They are, interestingly enough for our purposes, a family: a father, a mother, the grown son of their marriage, and the mother's two children from a second marriage. It turns out that the husband encouraged his wife's second marriage and then got back with his wife after her second husband died. All of this does not come out immediately. Some of it doesn't come out until the last few lines of the play. Neither does the hinted incest of the father and his voluptuous half-daughter or the accidental killing of one of the children by one of the others. All of these *content* facts, however, are really rather irrelevant to the *process* of the play.

In the play, six characters, born from Pirandello's imagination but left without a stage, invade the rehearsal of another Pirandello play seeking a plot. They want the stage manager to give them existence, as it were, by putting on their story. The play that ensues, however, is not their story. It is rather their refusal to accept the way the actors portray their roles, as well as the manner in which each one refuses to accept the way the others try to "re-cast" his or her own life. Throughout, the six characters interact with one another and with the actors who are trying to "act out" their lives. The actors themselves get caught up in a parallel plot mirroring what the six characters are doing. The effect on the audience after a while is to make it almost impossible to distinguish between illusion and reality. The play winds down like a broken clock and everybody throws up their hands at the end and walks off the stage.

During the play, the audience, caught up in the action that is continually interrupted by the actors or characters, wishes the interrupting would stop so that the play can continue. But, of course, the interruption of the play *is* the play and not a play within a play. *Six Characters* may best be described as a paradox within a paradox.

Pirandello describes how he decided to present these characters:

"Why not," I said to myself, "present this highly strange fact of an author who refuses to let some of his characters live though they have been born in his fantasy, and the fact that these characters, having by now life in their veins, do not resign themselves to remaining excluded from the world of art? And so let them go where dramatic characters do go to have life: on a stage. And let us see what will happen.... What have I rejected of them? Not themselves, obviously, but their drama, which doubtless is what interests them above all but which did not interest me. And what is it for a character — his drama? This drama is the character's *raison d'être,* his vital function, necessary for his existence. In these six, I have accepted the 'being' without the reason for being."

Pirandello's experience with the dependency and contrariness of his characters, as well as his ambivalence about their lessened need for him as the director of their lives, is not that dissimilar from that of the therapist. Our characters also come in asking us for a plot. Many is the time I have suggested to my "cast" that they try to act their lines differently only to receive as response, "But I can't; it would be totally out of character." The most important parallel, however, has to do with the fact that all our "productions" are paradoxical. The great paradox of therapy is that the patient speaks aloud: "I want you to help me with such and such problem, and I will pay you your fee." And then, in an aside: "But I'll do every damn thing in my power to prevent you from succeeding."

Written today, after having learned about counterparadox, Pirandello might have ended *Six Characters* differently. The contemporary conclusion would be that all the actors, unhappy with the script he forced upon them, would get together and sue him for malpractice. He, however, working in Rome (which is less than a day's ride from Milan), would have trumped in the end by adding an epilogue in which they are forced to hold a cast party one night a week.

Historical note: The work of Pirandello also creates a paradox for the entire world of family therapy, generally so concerned with family history and tradition. It has failed almost completely to recognize this ancestor and his "proximity" to Milan; Mareno (the creator of psychodrama), on the other hand, and perhaps the real link between the two, freely admitted his debt to this Nobel Laureate.

Scene VI / Theater of the Absurd: Waiting for Godot

This is a paean to ambiguity. Twenty-five years ago the Rand Corporation published a thick book that contained no words, only figures, orders of numbers which their computers assured them were totally free of hidden sequences so that scientists could put them into their equations without the worry that their results would be skewed by unseen patterns. I have always thought that this effort by scientists to assure lack of certainty was an ironic metaphor of our century. For in what period of world history has humankind been more bent on accurate information, and what era therefore was more in danger of devaluing ambiguity, which is not only essential for art but also for play and learning?

I have lived in the Washington area for twenty-five years. I also lived here for six months at the height of the McCarthy era in 1953. I've been part of the anxiety of looking for communists, the anxiety of looking for carcinogens, the anxiety of the Cuban missile crisis, the anxiety of Watergate, the anxiety of gas lines and inflation. During this time, I have witnessed the breakdown of certainty and the traditional sources of comfort. All conventions have been subverted. After Vietnam and Iran one realized that not only does might not make right, it no longer even makes might. Religion, too, has lost its ability to supply answers, except the fundamentalist branches that have instead lost the ability to tolerate questions. Perhaps it is not that God is dead: She has just gone into dysfunction because of the overfunctioning of the clergy.

Theater, like therapy, is a part of the culture of its time. So in times that are absurd, we have a theater of the absurd. In many ways the terribly ambiguous plays of Writer and Beckett and Ionesco break more with the certainty of theatrical tradition than even Pirandello. The latter at least had a message. But the message of the theater of the absurd is that there is no message, no clear answers to life's dilemmas.

All through watching Samuel Beckett's *Waiting for Godot*, which is considered the prototypical absurdist play, I kept thinking of the patient's wait in a therapist's anteroom, which, after all, is not so different from waiting for Godot. Godot, of course, like the Messiah (though unlike the therapist), never arrives. The disappointment does not lead, however, to an end of hoping, just the recognition that no one can bail you out. The theater of the absurd has been panned for denigrating hope, but I believe it's more a revolt against answers. It has been blamed for being unnecessarily tragic, but I believe it is saying that an ounce of persistence is worth a pound of valium.

One test for how effectively any family therapist is functioning (and how high the level of anxiety) may well be the proportion of questions he or she asks compared to the number of answers solemnly intoned. The effort to phrase the question relevantly has a natural superiority over trying to find the right answer. Answers constantly change but the basic questions of life do not, and questions more than answers reflect perceptions. They reveal modes of thinking, since the way the question is phrased already determines the range of answers that can be conceived. And for similar reasons, they have far more subversive power than answers to overthrow institutionalized mindsets.

A psychiatrist named John Kafka once wrote that not only are double messages schizophrengenic; so are their complete absence. To me. the hallmark of the schizophrenic thought process is the total incapacity to tolerate any ambiguity whatsoever. The great irony of psychotherapy in our lifetime is that, carried to its logical conclusion, seeking total knowledge of one's own dull mind shows the same absurd incapacity as the schizophrenic to tolerate ambiguity.

Epilogue:
Apocalypse Now, or Later

When my son was about eight he ingenuously (at least I hope it was ingenuously) got into the habit of setting me up for paradox by asking for everything in the negative: "I don't suppose I could have candy/pizza/

soda?" I found that his way of asking always created in me the urge to say, "Of course, you can have candy/pizza/soda." Realizing what was happening, I said to him, "I don't like the way you have begun to ask for things. I want you to ask for them straight. In fact, every time you ask for something in a negative way, the answer is 'no' in advance." So far, so good.

A few nights later, we sat down for a dinner that featured peas as the main vegetable. My son hates all vegetables genetically, but of all vegetables, the one he hates most is peas. Walking in and observing the fare, with neither a pause or nary a twinkle, he looked at me and asked, "I don't suppose I could have any of those peas, could I?"

One of the problems with an overfocus on technique in any activity is that eventually the opposition learns the counter-moves. It is as true in football (where every few years they change the rules to allow the offense or the defense to catch up), as in the arms race (radar jamming devices to jam the anti-jamming devices that stop up the jamming of the radar devices). It is a factor in evolution: the survival of DDT-proof mosquitos creates a need for new approaches to insecticide. Similarly, patient populations, like new generations of any other laboratory animal, eventually develop collective resistance to the latest surefire therapeutic intervention. This is probably why each new form of therapy works best when it first comes out. All focus on methods, whether it is method-acting or method-therapy, has its limits. It both shapes an opposition and dulls the imaginative capacity.

Families can no more be "fixed" than plays can be outlined. Arthur Miller dubbed the literal preoccupation with what-happens-next in a play the "caveman element," as in: "9 o'clock, Channel 8, *King Lear* (Drama). A mad old king is duped by his daughters." Given the various complexities, conflicts, and subtleties of any family's existence over a span of time, is the average "case history" any more profound than the *Lear* of the *TV Guide?*

There is also a caveman element in therapy. It surfaces in the emphasis on "pointing out the problem." It shows up in the myriad of successful cases presented in our conference theaters, and it colors all the miraculous cure stories told in our journals. But mostly it is the fabric of our belief that change comes about automatically when we finally figure out how to say the thing right.

It was precisely out of the struggle to fight such reductionism that theater was born. For therapy to speak to people profoundly, it must recognize that communication is much more than a set of linguistic procedures. Unquestionably the right line delivered at the right moment with the right sense of timing can transform a family's drama and shift their perspective. Certainly awareness does seem to come in flashes. But it is the preparing of the scene for those moments, the time and care that goes into the development of the plot that most distinguishes the playwright and therapist from the orator and the educator. When words are used with that deeper understanding, whether the context is theater or therapy, they have far less in common with prose than with poetry.

In entitling this essay "The Play's the Thing" I had in mind to convey that in any "theater," an emotional process, which takes time, always has the power to override diction or ideas, or to give them eloquence.

Good drama is not a function of clever words. And like all processes, whether it is baking, gardening, or healing, it is a child of the experience of time. Time is the father of joy and pathos, tragedy and seriousness, irony and mischievousness, paradox and madness, and absurdity and love. Most comparisons of theater and therapy overlook this common organizing principle so essential to the flowering of human creativity.

One of the great ironies of our profession may be that when Mareno created psychodrama he was concerned to take advantage of this connection between theater and therapy, but somehow the result has been to turn theater into prose. For his followers have taken theater out of therapy much as psychiatry took psychology out of medicine. It is not necessary to stage things in order to stage them.

Finally, the history of theater also has something to say about research. Recently at a national family therapy conference I heard a dramatic presentation of three new promising approaches to schizophrenia. After the show I happened to be listening in on two wizened founders of our movement as one sardonically said to the other, "Everything works with schizophrenia."

I was at that moment reminded of a comment made by Bernard De-Voto, an important literary critic of the 1940s, who was concerned about the effects on aesthetics of the new Marxist realism that evaluated art purely in terms of its social message — that is, its results, its function.

DeVoto said that the ultimate test of any form of criticism is not its insightfulness into a few plays, but the standards it establishes for future creativity.

Something similar may be said about all therapy and research: the ultimate test of any methodology is not whether it seems to have worked in some specific situations but whether you can take something away from that experience that has enriched your understanding and your appreciation of life.

Seven

EMPATHY DEFEATS THERAPY

An Interview with Helen Gill

GILL: *I understand you recently conducted a family therapy workshop for U.S. Army generals. Is the army receptive to family systems concepts?*

FRIEDMAN: More than I could have ever guessed. My original idea was to make a presentation on how fusion in a leader's family system at home could affect the clarity of command decisions in the field, but it turns out that the whole army is enmeshed in family matters.

What do you mean?

It seems that in order to have a volunteer army, the government has sweetened the pie by letting soldiers bring their families to Europe. So there are two hundred thousand troops in Germany and three hundred thousand dependents. Now every time a commander makes an ordinary decision affecting the movement of troops, he is instantaneously churning up family process, if not stepping into what's already churning. And all this does not take into account the generals' own families, particularly their wives, who are getting caught up in triangles with the colonels' wives.

It sounds very much like what you have written concerning ministers and congregations.

Or CEOs at IBM. It's remarkable. I developed some theories about how ministers' stress is the result of their being caught in the confluence of parishioner families, the church "family," and their own family, and now I find this theory also applies to a Panzer division.

First published in *Family Therapy News* (September–October 1988): 9.

What is an example of the process?

A good one would be the way emotional triangles sabotage change and keep things chronic. Towards the end of the second day with more than thirty generals, one wearing three stars and head of an entire army corps — two tank divisions — gets up and says to me, "One of our major problems is getting the sergeant-majors to stop getting the enlisted men out of bed in the morning. We try to tell them that approach is not going to make the EMs responsible in the field." And he turns to his fellow commanders and says, "But based on what Ed is teaching us here about emotional triangles, we're not going to have any more luck changing the sergeant-majors than they are in changing the enlisted men."

So we're all stuck?

Sometimes it seems that way, but I think the real stuckness is in our civilization and not in an institution or a given family. One of the most enlightening experiences of my life has been what I have observed over the past three years, in which I've been given the unique opportunity to conduct workshops for every possible branch of the helping professions: therapists, the medical community, teachers, lawyers, each major religious denomination, and now the military. I have found that each group thinks its problems belong to its profession, but the truth of the matter is that they are really all dealing with the very same issues phrased in the buzz words of their own particular discipline. Everybody is dealing with the same dilemma.

Which is?

That in every institution of our society, whether religious, health, educational, legal, or military, it always seems to be the most recalcitrant and the least motivated people who are calling the shots. Everywhere I go, I hear the same complaint. The dependent people, whether clients or staff, are in charge. The adaptation is in the wrong direction: a disproportionate amount of time, energy, money, and concern is being spent on those who will do the least with it. The strengths of our species are being diluted by this focus on pathology. Not the meek but the weak are inheriting the earth. It's counter-evolutionary.

That doesn't sound very empathic.

Funny you should mention that, because I think it is precisely our focus on empathy that is one of the major factors that has everybody stuck. It's a post–World War II emphasis. The word doesn't even appear in the original *Oxford English Dictionary* published in 1932. It first shows up as a human relations concept in the 1970s version.

What would you emphasize instead?

Responsibility. My whole life has been dedicated towards feeling for others, but we have a word for that. It's called compassion. Ironically, empathy is a self-defeating concept. For empathy to function in a way that is good for others, it must come out of someone who is well-defined. But the concept of empathy has wound up encouraging everyone to lose their own boundaries, so it works against the very self-regulation that is necessary for it to be employed objectively. That is how empathy plays into the hands of those who are least willing to take responsibility for their own emotional being or destiny. Put more simply, most therapists are too sensitive to be effective. In therapy emotional fusion with another is far more destructive than lack of concern or understanding.

So do therapists need insensitivity *training?*

I believe it is the focus on empathy rather than responsibility that has created the incredibly stressful triangle in all the helping professions whereby the motivated person winds up responsible for another (client, staff person, or family member) and their problem. This is the real source of burnout, not hard work.

That sounds more like a preacher talking than a therapist.

It just astounds me that there exists this notion that the best way to help people mature is to *feel* for them. Actually, religious institutions are the worst offenders at encouraging immaturity and irresponsibility. In church after church some passive-aggressive member of the congregation is holding the whole system hostage, and no one wants to fire him or force her to leave because it wouldn't be "the Christian thing to do." But this has nothing to do with Christianity. Synagogues also tolerate abusers because to get rid of them wouldn't be "the Christian thing to do." You know, at one point I asked a general, "Would it be correct to say that you have less trouble killing the enemy than firing a subordinate?" and he answered, "Sure, you don't have to see the whites of their eyes." Or, to go back to religion again, recently I was asked to consult with one of the major Protestant denominations in America about a plan to raise $50 million to help their most troubled and dysfunctional ministers. I responded by asking, "Why do you assume that such an investment in the dysfunctional would benefit your denomination more than if you put $50 million into your best?"

That's pretty radical.

It does get to the root of things. My favorite biblical story is the one about the golden calf. Aaron, feeling for the anxiety of the people while Moses has disappeared up the mountain to search for truth, gives them the valium of that day — an idol. The distinction between Moses and Aaron, the prophet and the priest, has characterized every helping profession ever since. It is only a small percentage of physicians, lawyers, and therapists who can tolerate enough pain in their clients to enable them, or challenge them, to grow. Most, like Aaron, want only to relieve their pain. But feeling pain has two dimensions to it, stimulus and threshold. That's obviously true concerning one's own self; the more motivated you are, the less you feel the pain. But with others, especially those who are dependent on you, when your threshold for their pain is too low then they can never learn to raise their own enough in order to change. The reason, by the way, that Moses has a higher threshold than Aaron for his people's pain is because Moses has vision.

And the moral is?

When members of the helping professions do not have personal goals for their lives — I mean aside from rescuing or helping others — they lose perspective on their clients, and then they can't distinguish their empathy from their anxiety.

Are you saying that the therapist's own development is more important than his or her techniques?

I'd hardly be the first to say that.

What else besides the emphasis on empathy do you see keeping the helping professions stuck in their ineffectiveness?

An unreasonable faith in reasonableness.

And is the answer paradox, or Kierkegaard?

Neither, or maybe both. I have been struck by how the thinking in the helping professions mirrors the thinking processes of the most impaired members of our species — the black-and-white characterizations, the either/or assumptions, the all-or-nothing responses, and the resulting efforts to will another to change. What schizophrenics can tolerate least is ambiguity. The resulting reductionist worldview leaves out a very essential characteristic of human existence, which is perversity. We do not necessarily work in our own best interest, no less those of another family member, even when we know what is right and want to. The failure to honor this dark dimension of human existence make everyone rigid and serious salvationists, puts us into enervating struggles with the resistance of our clients, and robs us of an important tool in upsetting pathological balance: mischievousness, particularly the kind that is challenging. I mean, why should the devil have all the fun?

Can you give an example of this?

Here's one from medicine that has ramifications for all the helping professions. I attended a biofeedback conference in which several physicians were talking about the importance of the patient's attitude and the use of imaging to help create the right perspective. Basically, I agreed with them. I've done a lot of thinking and writing about the idea that the hostility of an environment is not proportional to the toxic elements within it, but rather to the organism's own response. However, the panel reduced everything to the black-and-white, either/or notion that only if you think correctly can you survive; if you quit, or are negative, you die. That certainly does not fit my experience, either with human perversity or the paradoxical complexities of life.

So I asked the panel, "Suppose someone came to you and said, 'I know what the end stage of my cancer is going to be like. I don't want to linger. I would like you to teach me how to image my cancer cells so that they will defeat my immunological system faster.' " Then I added, "Assuming you were successful, would the patient really die faster or would you trick them into such self-regulation that they could be cured?" Well, the panel was completely nonplussed by the question (the audience loved it) and gave responses like, "I would never do that, it's unethical." That's precisely the kind of serious, salvationist view of life that subverts our healing efforts. And when that attitude is exhibited by the therapist, we teach both family members and leaders of organizations that they can change others by simply talking to their brains, which has yet to happen on this planet. The colossal error of modern psychotherapy, and perhaps also of education and religion, is the failure to accept the fact that reasoning and insight only work with people who are motivated to change.

Eight

THE BIRTHDAY PARTY

*An Experiment in Obtaining Change
in One's Own Family*

It is thought by many that anyone who engages in the practice of individual therapy would benefit, both personally and in his work, from
experiencing such therapy himself. Can the same be said for those who
practice family therapy? My guess is that, in fact, many who practice
family therapy with their patients are often tempted to use their skills and
insights to try to obtain change in their own families. Perhaps the family
therapist may be said to be in a perpetual multiple family group as he
draws parallels and refers insights back and forth between relationships
in his own family and those in the families with which he works.

To work therapeutically with one's own family could be the concealed
expectation of the family, and a major force in drawing the therapist to
that kind of professional work. After all, if patients are to be seen as
symptoms of their family networks, why not therapists? We talk about
identified patients; why not talk about *identified therapists?* I shall come
back to this idea more explicitly later.

This essay will describe a studied, carefully planned attempt to obtain
change in my own extended family over a two-year period, the focal
point or fulcrum for the whole process being a surprise birthday party for
my mother on the occasion of her seventieth birthday. First, I will give a
brief description of the extended network in which I wished to see change
occur, pinpointing those areas where I felt dysfunctional symptoms of
the network could be identified. Second, I will recount how I tried to

First published as "The Birthday Party: An Experiment in Obtaining Change in One's Own
Family," *Family Process* 10 (1971): 345–359.

encourage the process of change with some exposition of the theory on which I based my own actions. And third, I will offer some afterthoughts and general conclusions about how the professional person may work within his own extended family to obtain change.

Let me begin by describing my extended family on my mother's side. The first generation had three children, two girls and a boy, who were born in Europe and came to America, where they produced fourteen offspring (all first-generation Americans). The sisters each had five children, the brother had four. My mother's generation of fourteen cousins, on the other hand, produced only twelve offspring, primarily in multiples of one! Four of my mother's cousins had no children (one never married), and only two of the remaining had more than one child. In each case, the two cousins who were the only members of their generation to have more than one child were the siblings who became most involved in their spouse's extended family — that is, they were most out of the system.

Some other interesting attributes of the system are these: all of my mother's first cousins at the time of the party were alive and in their seventies except for her younger brother, who was sixty-eight, and the oldest cousin, who had committed suicide twenty-five years previously. Furthermore, in each of the three sets of siblings that made up my mother's generation, the sisters had stuck together. My mother and her older sister live on the same floor of the same apartment house in New York City. The two sisters in the Chicago group also live in the same apartment house. All four are widows, having lost their husbands around the age of fifty-five to sixty. None remarried. My mother and aunt, however, had had almost no contact with the Chicago cousins and had never met the younger one. The other two sisters from the New York group have lived within walking distance of one another on the northern tip of Manhattan throughout their entire lives. They have never had children, and they have never become widows!

It should be noted also that in the middle set of my mother's cousins, the two boys have always lived together, the youngest of that set living with his married brother in California. In contradistinction to this pairing off among siblings in my mother's generation, their children live almost totally separate lives from one another. It is true that they are cousins and not siblings, but generally speaking it can be said that the cousins on my level are almost never in communication with one another.

There were three points in this family network where I wished to see change, that is, where I felt pathological symptoms of the network were showing up. One was my own relationship with my mother, which I felt was distant and rigid despite many efforts on my part to be closer to her. The second concerned my oldest cousin's son, who started taking drugs at thirteen, was obese, and was doing poorly in school, in contrast to his older sister, who was bright, witty, and charming. The third place I wanted to see change was with regard to the younger of the two New York City cousins, who, despite the fact that he was an extremely successful professional person, was indeed the only unmarried member of my generation.

The Process

Since my own work with families is at the systems end of the continuum rather than the analytic, I should like to begin this section by indicating my conceptual approach to family systems. By "systems" I mean a set of relationships which, upon achieving homeostasis, functions to maintain that homeostasis through inner-adjusting compensations. Change in one relationship of a system so defined will usually bring about change in another relationship.

When it comes to family systems, I do not equate the degree of physical distance with the degree of emotional distance. People certainly are involved in important nonfamily relationship systems, but I think those other systems are rarely as intense emotionally as the family system, so that a family relationship that is physically distant can be much more influential than a nonfamily relationship of greater physical proximity. The potential for becoming free from the influence of one's family system, however, is much greater in an approach that brings one towards the family than in an approach that takes one away. I think, therefore, in terms of differentiation of self *within* the system rather than independence of it, and do not believe it is really possible to become independent of one's family system except by becoming intensely part of another system (and then all one has succeeded in doing is transferring the dependency).

Success at achieving such differentiation of self can be measured, I believe, in the extent to which one can be a part of the family without automatically being one of the "emotional dominoes." The path towards such a goal can be achieved best not by a process of internal analysis of oneself but through a process of external perceptions that analyze the system. In other words, I do not think in terms of a *sense* of self, which seems too unverifiable, but in terms of a *position* of self.

In my work with my family of origin and with clinical families, my primary orientation is Bowen theory. Also, I have been influenced by an approach to general systems thinking known as "black box" theory. As computers and other sophisticated electronic equipment became too complex to take apart when they dysfunctioned, an attempt was made to deal with this by inserting new inputs into the system instead of trying to analyze the dysfunctional elements. The method is not all that hit-or-miss, since one always knows some of the major characteristics of the system (contained, but unseeable) within the "black box." Some of the ramifications of that approach are to see dysfunctional parts as always symptomatic, to define dysfunction always in interrelational terms, to note that the definition or label of dysfunction also includes a large measure of perspective, and to diminish the distinction between essence and function.

One other fact has influenced my decision to apply black box theory to human beings and their family systems. Miniaturization with computers has reached the point that ten thousand elements can be put on a disk one-tenth of an inch square. By the end of the decade that should be increased to a hundred thousand. To achieve the density of cells in the human brain one would need a cubic inch of the latter. Thus I have been asking myself, if less complex systems than human relationships are now being considered too complex to change through methods that analyze the components (or even the relationships sometimes), surely a similar approach is worth considering in trying to obtain change in families.

Applying black box theory to my own family, I began asking what seemed most to characterize the program of my own family system's set of relationships. How could I go about changing some of the most significant inputs, at least some of my own?

What struck me most about my mother's extended family was the set pattern of relating; the isolation of the cousins, the closeness among my mother's cousins of the sets of siblings — with little crossing of lines there. Within my mother's sibling group alone I was struck by the fact that my mother herself was like Cinderella before the ball — she had been given the job of taking care of *their* mother in her seventies, when she was old and feeble and defecating in our bathtub because she was too blind and unaware to know where she was. I also decided that the biggest "no-no" in the family — perhaps because no one was dying — was age; I took note of my own relative disengagement; I noticed also that I was almost the only member of my family in the "helping" professions.

In these terms the question was, what would be the most "unthinkable" event one could carry out in this family system? Obviously, to give a birthday party — indeed a surprise birthday party — a ball for Cinderella, so to speak, outside of New York City, and given by the last person the family might have expected to throw a ball.

Planning the Birthday Party

For three months, therefore, I set about calling every one of my mother's cousins and siblings — from top down, in deference to age. Her sister, as you can imagine, was against it — until I put her in charge of something. Added and unexpected benefits came during this phase, as in conversation with each relative I had to ask information about the others. I received the information in the form of opinions I did not expect but made sure to pass on to the others when I called them. It was as though there were little light bulbs connected into each circle and square on the family diagram that were either all out or all on (steady state sort of thing); the day I started telephoning those bulbs started flashing — out of phase — for the first time in many, many years. Something dormant (and apparently dead) came to life.

One interesting detail during this part of the process may be mentioned. When I called the oldest group of cousins, living in Manhattan, the brother said they couldn't come because one of his sisters was very sick but he would tell his sisters for me and I needn't call. I then called the sister who wasn't sick, who said she couldn't come because her sister was very, very sick, and she would tell her for me; I needn't call her sister. (Now remember it was this brother's son who was unmarried.) When I spoke to the sick sister, I found her much brighter and much more knowledgeable about family than the other two — this certainly fit all my ideas about families, namely, that it couldn't be clear at all who was sick for whom and indeed the symptomatic one was often the most aware and responsible one. So I wrote her a short note saying I was sorry they all couldn't come down for the day and I realized that she had a responsibility to keep the family together, but how would we ever get Vicky (my unmarried cousin) married? As I calculate, that letter arrived in New York on a Friday, and the following Monday Vicky called to accept the invitation and asked if he could bring a girl.

With the exception of Vicky, none of my mother's cousins was able to come nor was any of her close friends whom I called — all, however, kept the secret, and all sent good wishes. To each person I had sent a list of the names of everyone invited. There were twenty-six people at the party, and the surprise was total. Only one of her siblings did not come, the next oldest brother. He, incidentally, married secretly when young, fifty-five years previously, and came back to live with the family for six months before he announced he was married. He was the only sibling who had two children and the only one from this group who had become more a part of his spouse's system. I point this out because it has become my experience generally to note with families that brothers and sisters will carry out interrelational inputs at age seventy as though they were still viewing one another at age seven.

There is one other grouping I should like to mention before talking about the party itself. One of my mother's intimates was not a blood relative but her sister-in-law on my father's side. This aunt and uncle had lived in Canada with their only child, a son, for forty years, had been extremely successful in the retail business, and were perhaps my nuclear family's closest relatives second to my mother's sister's family. In recent years this aunt had been sickly, alcoholic, and depressed, and had growths on her feet that necessitated repeated operations. At any given time, however, she was liable to recover completely from everything and take a trip halfway around the world. When my father died, this aunt and uncle had begged my mother to move to Canada to be near them.

The Canadian group also would not come to the party because my aunt had become phobic after she finally stopped drinking. And, like the group in northern Manhattan, none dared fly away for a day "to the heat of Washington." I learned as much about those who did not come to the party as those who did. For example, the absurd excuses given by this group and the one in northern Manhattan made their own stuck-togetherness stand out in relief and pointed out directions for follow-up in the future.

The Party

The birthday party itself was a complete success, especially considering the logistics. People came from four cities and had to meet at one place at precisely the right hour while my mother was bluffed into going out for an hour. The caterer was precision itself, arriving and setting everything up during the same time. Actually, I felt the success at keeping the secret — that is, the ease with which I was able to get my family to gang up in a conspiracy against my mother — did not speak well for my family. Her total surprise, however, confirmed my feeling that I had done something truly unthinkable.

At the party one event in particular was significant. My next older cousin, my mother's sister's son, had been like a complementary sibling to me. Although Walter Toman, in his work entitled *Family Constellations,* recognizes the complementary aspects of sibling relationships, he says only-children are "wild cards."[1] It has been my experience generally that if there is enough feedback between their parents, two only-children from the same family will produce some kind of complementary system. My cousin is an accountant, very proper in all ways, no maverick opinions, and superresponsible for our two mothers. He became totally, helplessly drunk within one hour after the party started and was walked around outside by his wife for the next three hours. During this time his son, whom I knew only to be obese and failing in school, told me he had been on hard drugs for the last two years. In the middle of the party, when I investigated a strange tinkle of breaking glass downstairs, I found my aunt, aged seventy-one, who in her concern for her intoxicated son had given our glass sliding door something like a karate chop with her knee as she went to look for him. She was uninjured, but the entire door had been shattered. Rushing in to keep the party going, I told everyone upstairs that they would never guess what my Aunt Rose had done to

---

1. W. Toman, *Family Constellation* (New York: Springer, 1967).

upstage my mother, her younger sister. Strangely, maybe because of the way I put it, nobody believed me and everyone went right on eating and drinking while my unmarried cousin, the dentist, applied iodine.

In the months that followed the party, the following events occurred in rather rapid succession:

- One month later my conservative accountant cousin had grown a beard, which for my aunt (who will clean your ash tray before you have finished your cigarette) was truly earth-shaking.

- I wrote him a letter telling him I thought growing a beard was a terrible thing to do to his mother, and whom would I look up to now?

- I wrote my young cousin a letter asking him seriously what his acid trips were like and received a long exposition about the effects of drugs on *coitus* — to use his word. He also announced that he had given up drugs because he wanted whole children.

- Two months later my mother's younger brother, the youngest in this line of cousins and the only one who had not reached seventy, dropped dead of a heart attack.

- His wife thereupon came to Washington six months later to live with her married daughter, and the younger cousin enrolled at George Washington University the following year.

- Precisely between those events, my dentist cousin married a Gentile divorcee with two children, the granddaughter of a prominent New York Protestant clergyman. They were to come to Washington for a private marriage ceremony to be performed by me, but his father had a heart attack, and they haven't made it yet.

During the following year my Canadian aunt made a suicide attempt with drugs. I wrote this aunt a letter, having been told by my uncle and cousin that she couldn't come to the phone. I told her that I had always thought of her as my most competent aunt and, considering her success in business over the years, I couldn't understand how she would do such a sloppy job of committing suicide. I followed that by describing my own life in the most depressing terms I could think of. As I say, I was encouraged to do this by what I had seen with the other group.

The reaction of my aunt was most interesting. As it turned out, my mother arrived in Ottawa two days after the letter. My aunt never revealed the contents, and to this day everyone is saying what a wonderful thing my mother's visit did for my phobic aunt, who had not left the house in two years and was now "back to her old self." Indeed, she has since struck up relationships with other relatives in the States and relates to me entirely differently than she does to anyone else. (It never ceases to amaze me that those who think of "systems" as a "cold" approach usually resort to electrical means when it comes to shock.) My aunt has also reestablished contacts with her own family of origin from which she had become increasingly cut off over the years. I paid a visit to her during the summer two months later, during which time she gave me "hell" for writing such a nasty letter; she came down to Washington to hear me preach (for the first time) during the High Holy days; she went to some weddings on her side of the family the following month. In December she told my uncle that she could no longer take their forty years of a battling marriage, their separate vacations, etc., and that his time she really was going through with their ten-year-old, *suspended,* but constantly threatened separation agreement. My uncle went off to the West Indies for a month and came back with cancer of the liver. He died two months later.

I have, since the party, kept up my own interests in the extended network, paying a trip to Chicago, for example, to visit my mother's and aunt's two girl cousins, and wound up in the ridiculous position of being questioned by my mother and aunt about the family for a change. They had never met the younger one, age seventy-two.

The Hangover

In this last section I should like to describe some of my thoughts and conclusions about doing work in one's own family. I shall subdivide this section into two parts: technical and personal.

From the point of view of technique I would say I consciously tried different varieties. Listing them in order of *least* effectiveness, I would say they were (1) being straightforwardly analytical about people or relationships, that is, being the expert; (2) telling them a story about one of my clients; (3) performing verbal reversals; (4) performing behavioral reversals; and (5) being stupid — this one has to follow, if being expert is at the other end of the scale.

Regarding the straightforward analytical approach, I found that the reaction was almost always one of denial. I was told I didn't understand, or a comment would be made about my playing therapist. On the other hand, when I went to Canada after my aunt's suicide attempt and spent one week with the family, never once making an interpretation, I found by the end of the week they got so scared by this that they began to talk to me in a way that showed they knew more, and thought more, in analytic terminology than I did.

Telling them about a client had some limited effectiveness. On several occasions since the party, when members of my family were deeply distressed about something, I found that telling them about a similar situation from my practice helped depersonalize the situation for them. It reminded me of what had worked and not worked with the client and thus helped me know how to behave at that moment. But most of all, I think, it enabled the conversation to continue with me in the position of experienced relative who was not trying to change them but who, from their point of view, despite his experience, didn't seem too anxious about it, either.

For example, for about a year my mother's older sister had been obsessed with anxiety about gastrointestinal problems. In her concern over the doctor's failure to find something specific, she had not been eating and was thus losing weight. The loss of weight contributed further to her worry that something sinister was at work. Everyone, including the family doctor, had been at a loss to reassure her. I had treated a similar case with a "paradoxical intention" barrage: did she know where the cancer was, what progress did she think it had been making, and, finally, people didn't just get cancer — she must have done something wrong and perhaps God was punishing her.

Thus I dealt with my aunt by: (1) not attempting any reassurance; (2) figuring, but not mentioning, that it had something to do with her son's involvement elsewhere (which indeed turned out to be the case); and (3) telling her as coldly as possible that I still needed her help in getting my mother straightened out, and I would appreciate it if she could just hang on a bit longer.

The third technique is verbal reversals. The two kinds I have employed most have been to out-kook and to go contrary to my instincts. An example of an out-kooking dialogue might go like this (with my dramatic aunt from Canada and in front of my mother, who always feels so sorry for her):

Aunt: Eddie, what do you think of me?

Me: I never analyze my relatives.

Aunt: I have opinions about you.

Me: Well, maybe you can get more distance.

Aunt: You must have some opinions.

Me: Okay, I think you're crazy, but it sure keeps you from being boring.

The other form of verbal reversal is to follow one's instincts and then do the opposite. Thus when my aunts, who are in their seventies, complain about their sundry ailments, and I find myself thinking, "They're old, afraid of dying, lonely, etc.," I immediately tell them they're getting older, or nobody lives forever. Sometimes before they get a chance to complain, say on the phone, I tell them they sound terrible. And then we usually have a delightful conversation. As my mother got close to retiring (at seventy-two), I would take her for a drive and point out the new old folks home and describe how secure she would be there. She is now looking for another job and applying for unemployment insurance!

The effect of the verbal reversal on these relationships is, I believe, that I convey I won't play their games. Consequently they relate in a much more adult manner to me than to those who take the so-called compassionate approach. I believe I sometimes set an example for other members of the family and make unthinkable actions doable.

The fourth technique, the real reversal, is more effective, I believe, though I must admit that this dichotomy between verbal and action reversals is somewhat artificial. There are two kinds here, also. One is to behave in a situation the way no one in the family ever does; the other is to behave the way you yourself never do. The party was so successful, I believe, because both things happened. I have been doing a lot of research on how widows should invest their money, and sending advice to my mother. My CPA cousin has always done my mother's income taxes — for free — and she naturally takes my very professional-appearing plans to him, who admits to my mother he hasn't done much thinking about this area. My final recommendations are always overly conservative, and he winds up having to suggest something more speculative in comparison.

Switching means of communication is another good behavior reversal (say phone and letter), but reversing whom one talks to about whom is better. Throughout my life I have had gossipy talks with my mother about my aunts; recently I have been doing this with my aunts about my mother. For example, my mother always took a highly sympathetic and supportive position towards my Canadian aunt despite years of my telling my mother that I thought she was selfish. I got a juicy tidbit from my aunt about how she thought my father secretly liked her and passed it on. My conversations with my mother now are filled with my mother's diatribes about my aunt as I try to explain that you have "to understand her." I find that the more I do this the freer my mother seems to be with me. (My grandfather died eight months after I was born, and I believe I replaced him in some original triangle with his two daughters.)

The best reversal I have found, however, is to refuse to be serious about what the family is most uptight about. I would add, however, that being exaggeratedly overserious sometimes seems to amount to the same thing. (I am also coming to believe there would have been much less possibility that my hypertensive father would have died at fifty-six if he could have taken my mother's "goodness" less seriously.)

This brings me to the fifth and I believe most powerful way of inducing change in one's family, and primarily I believe because it focuses us most on our own input, and that is what I call being stupid. At the beginning of this essay I raised the question: if patients were to be considered symptoms of their family system, why not therapists? Maybe the same processes that produce dysfunction create other kinds of functioning. Sometimes when a member of a family becomes the patient, the other members respond in a way that keeps that person in the patient role, even though it is ultimately to their own detriment. Maybe a similar process goes on regarding professionals and their families: once someone becomes a member of the helping professions the effect on the family is to have them adapt to that person in ways that are not necessarily helpful to that person or themselves. If this is true, then the way to get the most change in the homeostasis of such a system is clearly never to play therapist in the system — that is, therapist as they would think of therapist, indeed to play anti-therapist (stirring up trouble, not being helpful or responsible, giving pain or at least not rushing in to relieve it).

All forms of reversal help in this matter, of course. I asked my formerly alcoholic aunt to take back a bottle of unusual Scotch as a gift to my cousin. She "forgot" it at my mother's in New York. Until my dentist cousin got married I never missed an opportunity to remind him of his responsibility to his aunts and parents as their only offspring. I have found, however, that asking stupid questions or making obvious commonsense interpretations of equally obvious pathological behaviors turns relatives into very insightful people. And that gets me asking, "Well, if they knew the answers all along, why the hell are they asking me about the problem?"

For myself as rabbi, another way I have found to be unprofessional is to fail to go to, no less to perform, weddings and funerals for members of the family. This is producing a very strong reaction; on the other hand, you can almost watch the shifts in responsibility among my cousins when I force my family members to find their own rabbis. For example, when I just couldn't make it to an uncle's funeral, another cousin (the oldest in the line) who went, took charge. This has changed his relationship with that uncle's family, and I believe had corresponding salutary effects on his own nuclear family.

I find this quite a paradox: that is, by *not* helping precisely where because of my professional expertise I could have been most helpful, I *may* have been more useful.

Now I should like to conclude with a few personal observations. This whole essay has been framed in terms of obtaining change in one's extended family. Yet I am quite sure that the person benefiting most from any attempt to induce such changes, at least in the ways I have been describing, is the person doing it. In fact, it would be my guess that if one sets about trying to induce the change, or for the sake of helping the relatives primarily, it won't work, or at least it won't work as well. The paradox here is resolved, I think, by remembering that as long as you are doing it for others you would be behaving as a therapist, a role that is hard to get out of and that secretly maintains homeostasis.

The approach I have been taking, therefore, is to do these things to see what it teaches me about my family. This in turn, however, has raised some interesting and serious theoretical questions. First of all, I have been wondering recently if these five techniques do not wind up with exactly the same effectiveness rating when one is working professionally with families. This is an exciting idea, for I have never been comfortable with a style of therapy that could not also be a style of life. Thus, I have begun to ask myself if what I have most in common with those who see me professionally is that we have both been the results of similar processes and that, therefore, the more I understand about my family and my position in it the more I will understand family process in general. These are insights I can share.

From the personal point of view I should also like to make a passing comment on what I have most obviously avoided, namely, the effect on one's nuclear family if one tries to obtain change in one's extended family. To talk publicly about relationships in this area is to get too personal; on the other hand, I would not want to imply, by ignoring that area, that there are no repercussions.

It may also be worth noting that my wife received several notes of thanks. This was quite surprising since I did not involve her in one single detail, having had the entire affair catered down to the silver-ware, chairs, and tables. All correspondence and phone calls to set up the party came only from me; no one had even spoken to my wife during the preparations.

Finally, I should like to enter a disclaimer. When this paper was delivered, some heard it as playing God and suggested that I should have warned my family about what I was trying to do. Let me state clearly, therefore, that I knew I could not be fully aware of the results. This is not to say I had no fears, trepidations, or fantasies. (None of my fantasies about deaths and suicides materialized — perhaps because fantasies come out of the system as it exists. If individuals are to be seen as symptoms of the family, so must their fantasies.) Things had been the way they had been for an awfully long time; members of the family were suffering now because of the irresponsibility, perhaps dependency, of others. I decided, therefore, I would take responsibility only for my own feelings and behavior and the other members of the family would have to take responsibility for theirs.

In no way, therefore, do I take credit for any of the changes I have described in my family, for in no way can I prove that my new inputs produced the new outputs. But I do believe that few of the things I did would have had the same effect on the family if anyone else would have done them, and if that is true, it is not because of any special attribute, talent, or personality factor that resides within me, but because of where I am on the family diagram.

Change in My Family — A Generation Later

A generation would appear to provide an adequate yardstick for measuring change in a family, in a societal "movement," or in a thinking person's thinking. However, it probably takes at least six generations to decide whether any change that occurs in family process is a fundamental change or the recycling of a symptom. In all events, two decades in the course of a family is enough time for a child to be born and leave home; for a marriage to mature and dissolve; for vibrant individuals to enter senility; for close relatives to become irreconcilably distant; for kin to be almost forgotten; for unquestioned expectations to be obliterated, or for undreamed-of surprises to materialize; for improbable connections to become connected; and for the seemingly impossible not only to become possible, but to be taken for granted. Almost all of these emotional phenomena occurred in my family since "the party."

Thinking about my mother's family of origin, how could I have predicted that the same family today, almost twenty years later, would include:

* my daughter, two years old at the time, now the deep-thinking fashion plate of her Deep South sorority;

* my sixteen-year-old son, four at the time, now playing with robots, repairing video arcade games, and rewiring our beach house for a hobby;

* my mother's entire generation gone, save for two of her first cousins, aged ninety and ninety-six, who have not seen one another for sixty

years, and only recently found out each still exists through my contacts with both of them;

- all my own older first cousins, still alive save one, the gentle son of my mother's gentlest (and oldest) brother, who gently killed himself in his office at the close of work one day with sleeping pills and a plastic bag;

- my CPA "drinking" cousin's attractive, intelligent daughter, who was *my* daughter's present age at that time, now, at thirty-eight, the emergency room director of a major metropolitan hospital.

Or was it predictable that my unmarried dentist second cousin would finally have gotten married and divorced (with custody of his daughter), and married again? Or that *his* only first cousin, whom I hardly knew, a childlike, childless, outdoors enthusiast, would be killed at age fifty on a bicycle by a jackknifing "semi," thus leaving the dentist and his on-the-verge-of-punk, fifteen-year-old daughter the only living branch on that part of the family tree?

I do remember, though, when they told my grandmother in 1949 that my cyclist cousin's mother, her favorite, superresponsible niece, had killed herself upon learning she had cancer (some say glaucoma), that her own mother, my grandmother's older sister, had assumed responsibility for my grandmother when *their* mother died two months after my grandmother's birth, leaving their widowed father — my grandmother once told me — to marry a shrew.

Nor could I have expected that my oldest first cousin, the only one in my branch who had been divorced, at twenty-five, would be divorcing again at age sixty-seven and remarrying within the year? Or that he would at that ripe old age first begin to move towards me after a generation of my pursuing him, now that he had finally left the wife with whom he had been fused for more than a generation? His father, incidentally, had been the only one of my mother's siblings not to come to "the party," because he had to go with his wife "to the mountains," although, in retrospect, his failure to attend was perhaps due to the fact that he wanted to avoid questions about his other child, his expatriate daughter, who had cut herself off from the family around that time in order to keep secret the fact that her brilliant, oldest son had been imprisoned for his own creative version of "the international drug trade." And who could have expected that a generation later she would now, along with her brother, be two of my closer kin, or that the former "jailbird" would now be the head of his own software consulting firm, no less that he would now be "in" and his brother, the physician, "out" because of the good doctor's marital choice; even as her father, "who went to the mountains," received similar treatment from our grandmother for his marital choice (her own mother) — and his choice at least was Jewish!

Nor could it have been foreseen that my favorite aunt (of the glass sliding door) would never forgive me till her dying day after she read "The Birthday Party" (even though reading it helped bring her expatriate niece back into the fold), creating a cutoff of such intensity that neither her son nor his children would ever relax with me again until her death. The cutoff was intensified — if such a thing were possible — when, in my mother's last years, they all fought all my efforts to keep my mother out of a nursing home, where they were convinced "she" would be more comfortable.

In some ways, some of this makes sense, but it is always possible to play such games of hindsight. Every family provides enough different directions for an observer to say the connections are apparent.

But are these the changes and connections that count? Is there any evidence that the next generation is better differentiated, any evidence that the physical or mental health of the family has changed, or its density been significantly affected, by what happened on that Bastille Day seventy years after my mother was born? There is absolutely none. But that is not the only conclusion to be drawn, for I have continued to work at relationships in my family of origin, throughout the passing of this generation — however, for a different set of reasons and with a very different rationale than I applied in 1968. In this respect there has been change — significant change. In 1968 most of my major motivation was to "help the family." There were pockets of fusion that I saw leading to severe symptoms. My major intent was to "disequilibrate" things. Over the years I gave up that self-important (or really no-self) view of saving others and reached a position of making all contacts simply for my own benefit and for the benefit of my children. I was an "only" with only "onlys" for first cousins. I understood all too well, both from my clinical experience and my family, the pernicious potential both for my children and for myself in that sort of isolation that tends to promote cutoffs, or their opposite, fusion. After all, the most cutoff branch of the family had the severest types of dysfunction for three successive generations. In this respect, I would claim to have succeeded to some extent in helping to derail what appeared to be a multigenerational trend. It has not been easy, and it has taken most of this past generation to understand and accomplish. Here are two examples of this change in approach, one from my father's side, and one from my mother's.

Change in My Own Thinking since "the Party"

Both my mother's and father's families of origin have tended to be explosive rather than implosive. With the deaths of my uncles and aunts, almost none of their children (my first cousins on either side) have remained in touch with one another, not that there has been any outright feuding or backbiting. They all simply drifted apart and became swallowed up in their own nuclear groupings. All very nice people. If some have met with violence, none have ever expressed it. Almost all have recovered from what has ailed them. Hardly anyone has died before the age of seventy from illness. And each, as I told him or her about my journeys to visit the others, has been genuinely interested in my reports — including, on my mother's side, a recent, first-time-ever visit to the Chicago branch, most of whom (generation five and six) were astounded to find they had relatives in New York. My efforts on both sides have included persistent pursuit, cross-country travel to nodal events, and refusal to be turned off by unintentional insults and, at the beginning, suspicion and argument.

On my father's side, I am the next to youngest of six male first cousins, the children of two brothers and two sisters, all now dead for more than a decade. Their parents (our grandparents) are buried in separate cemeteries in Brooklyn and Queens, though no one knows why. We live on a perimeter that is circumscribed by Hawaii, California, Ohio, Canada, Washington, D.C., and Florida. We range in age from fifty-three to seventy. I have been the only one to retain contact with each of the other five. Over the past ten years I have made sure to visit all of them as I traveled to their area, in one instance persevering carefully and patiently to rework a cutoff with the closest cousin from my youth by purposefully getting into a triangle with his reclusive mother, and having our children "jet-set" visit. With regard to another "distant" cousin, I once rearranged a speaking engagement so that I could travel cross-country to his son's wedding, making sure to bear good wishes from the others (I called them all beforehand) and bearing back similar greetings when I told them all about the "lovely affair" upon my return. Six months later, he worked out a similar way of attending my son's Bar Mitzvah. And, on that occasion, *for the first time in the family's history,* a representative of each of my father's siblings (four of the six offspring) gathered in the same place at the same time! I did not have to point that fact out to the others, all suddenly turned photographer. Some had not seen each other in more than thirty years. Not only that, soon after they planned what amounted to an international cousins' reunion, saying, "Isn't it a shame that the next generation has never met?" It took place in Florida, after a year of negotiation about the site, and all six first cousins came. We had never been all together before. I prepared a six-generation family diagram for distribution before the event. They are now planning a second reunion on the west coast so that the next generation who could not afford the trip east could meet.

On my mother's side, the greatest cutoff, as I said, had been with my aunt and her son and his children — in many ways most painful. This is the part of the family with whom I had been closest from earliest childhood. My aunt had been a second mother to me since her mother lived with us, and she often came to visit. I had officiated at the funeral of her husband (my favorite uncle) and had delivered the talk at her grandson's Bar Mitzvah, and I had always liked his older sister (the emergency room physician). However, no effort, from nonchalant surprise telephone calls to genuine letters, or reports about the doings of other family members, brought any change in their view of me as cruel for the way I kept my mother out of a nursing home. In fact, they could not tolerate being in the same room with me, all pointedly avoiding my daughter's Bat Mitzvah the year after my mother died. Finally, I just gave up, but did not reciprocate the cutoff; cutoffs take *two*. I stopped trying but was able emotionally to keep the door open, and said to others, "I will just have to wait till she dies."

When my aunt did die, my cousin, now having experienced for a year what I had experienced with his aunt's death, and finding himself aping my determination to keep her out of a nursing home, called me immediately. With a soft, familiar, loving voice I had not heard in twenty years, he asked if I would do the funeral. I jumped at the chance, and when he and his children begged out of my suggestion that they do the eulogy, delivered my own, anecdotal and with warm humor praising her foibles and her overfunctioning. I had been sure to bring my whole family with me. My son, now almost thirteen, was practically the same age that my cousin's son was the last time we had been friends at "the party," twenty years before. As this former Fulbright scholar in stage design drove us to the airport, he engaged my son, seated next to him (I had carefully taken a backseat) in the same kind of elder-mentor relationship I had had with him when he had come of age. They all came to his Bar Mitzvah two months later.

One last event is particularly worth noting. Three years ago, I spent a day visiting two cemeteries, one in New Jersey, where my parents are buried, one "across the bridge" in Queens, where my mother's parents have lain, unvisited, for more than thirty years. It was the first time since my grandmother's funeral that I had visited, even though she had been my roommate for the first fourteen years of my life. She had moved in when I was a newborn, since her husband, my grandfather, had died eight months after I was born. I had always assumed that my position in the family's triangle was due to that "transference." It had never occurred to me that if that was the significant replacement in my prepartum past, it did not explain why I also felt so close to my grandmother's sister's children, or those from my grandmother's brother's branch. They, after all, were only my grandfather's in-laws!

At the cemetery that day I read my grandmother's father's name, Avigdor, for the first time (though I once used it in a short story, not knowing where I had gotten it). As I stood looking down, some long-unthought-of associations returning to my consciousness, I suddenly realized that it was he, my great-grandfather, whom I had replaced in my anointing grandmother's life; he had been the *scholar,* my grandfather only a *tailor.* It was this widower, who had lost his own wife in the birth of his youngest daughter, my grandmother, who with her siblings fled *not* the pogroms but the shrew. When I told the tale to Murray Bowen, he said, "Ed, it's been a long time coming." Four years later I am now beginning to realize it was really only the beginning.

Both the power of multigenerational transmission as well as its ability to disguise itself will now be documented in a scientific manner. Only after I wrote all this and observed the family history for the hundredth time did the following facts become clear to me.

Three characteristics of the multigenerational transmission process stand out on the maternal side of the family. Most striking is that the descending order of dysfunction remains intact from the first down to the fifth generation. Members of that generation, on the other hand, with only one exception, are not only all reproducing "from generation to generation," but have all also tended to do very well professionally. Only one member of that branch has failed to reproduce, although one in the next generation is unmarried at thirty-eight. It is generally a good rule of thumb when studying family history that if the younger siblings are doing better in life than their older sisters and brothers, the dysfunction came into the system early and was as if "absorbed" by the older children. The child who loses her mother in childbirth will not suffer the same trauma as her older siblings who have already established a bond. The most significant fact, however, is not that this occurred in the 1870s, but that its residue seems to be around in the 1980s.

A second significant characteristic of the family is its tendency to stay together, as well as an apparent correlation between infertility and moving away from a family center. This correlation between geographical distancing from the family and failure to reproduce can be seen in generations three, four, and five. Speaking for myself, I also moved away and did not become a parent until age thirty-four (after completing five years of psychoanalysis!). I am almost the only member of any branch who keeps in touch with members of the other branches. This may be related to my position as the emotional replacement for the founding father, Avigdor, and may also help explain my emphasis within the family therapy movement on the importance of nodal events.

A possible third characteristic of the multigenerational transmission process has to do with untimely death and the names of family members beginning with "L." My great-grandmother, who died in childbirth, was named Lilith, and each of her children gave at least one of their children a name that began with "L." In 1980 (a century after the death of their great-grandmother), within a six-month period two of the children of those so "honored" died, and a third came very close, although none of the three had any knowledge of the misfortune of the others. One died at age fifty-two, by accident; the second age fifty-five, by suicide; I was the one who came close — at the age of forty-eight I needed immediate bypass surgery. What makes the above pattern so unusual is that in all three branches of the family and throughout all six generations (eighty people), untimely death is extremely rare. It is, of course, too farfetched to assume that such family emotional history helps explain my habitual use of the term *dybbuk,* and *demon,* in my teaching over the years when referring to the uncanny persistence of families in resisting change.

Other Changes in My Thinking

The following are some conclusions I have reached about family of origin work based on my continued experience with my own family, my coaching of clients with their families, and my supervision of other therapists during the generation since "the party."

1. The primary purpose for all work in one's family of origin has to be for oneself, and it cannot be just in the service of self-differentiation — one has to get a kick out of it.

2. Families can come together again even after a generation of distance, and sometimes only after a generation has passed or has "passed away."

3. For the distance in that time-space continuum to be bridged, however, there must be a catalytic family member prepared to take advantage of catalytic family moments. Such a "family leader" must love his family, have a genuine desire to be with (at least some of) them, and possess a sense of responsibility that enables him or her to resist resistance. Yet that sense of responsibility cannot be borne so seriously that it destroys his or her ability to introduce the playful and sometimes downright ludicrous initiatives that are necessary for maintaining a nonanxious presence.

4. Accomplishing this task takes years. Processes must be allowed to develop so that the watchful eye can take advantage of the crises and turn them into opportunities. The task cannot be willed, though serendipity will help. In short, the involvement must be

relegated to the "back burner" of a lifetime project rather than being given the priority of something to be accomplished in the near future.

5. The importance of nodal events, family reunions of any type, and rites of passage cannot be underestimated. They were our species' own natural device for dealing with change and separation, the two major goals of all activity that has come to be called "therapy." They are, in fact, the original form of all therapy, and began, indeed, as family therapy.[2]

6. The effort as described above will have major effects on the intellectual and professional development of the "leader," whether or not he or she is a "therapist." Chief among them will be increased clarity on all issues of life; second is a broadened capacity to deal with anxiety, anxious situations, and anxious people not obtainable through any other human endeavor; and third is an ability to think process and disdain technique that makes all other forms of training and supervision appear superficial.

7. The power of family process is awesome. Its capacity to resist efforts to mold it into other forms, change its direction, or stop it in its tracks is all but beyond human potential. It is also a wily cat that cannot be fooled and, indeed, will put to its own service all efforts to lead it astray. It can, however, be skinned in another direction.

8. That other direction develops when the family member with the most motivation to help his or her family change (whether he or she comes by this because of his or her family position or because of an understanding of family process) works primarily to keep himself or herself from being zapped by the family emotional system, while remaining in touch. It is success in that direction that can have a ripple effect, sometimes leading to change — but *not* if you even try to keep that potential benefit in mind.

9. To the extent all of the above is correct, then what Murray Bowen has been trying to teach this past generation differs so

2. See E. H. Friedman, "Systems and Ceremonies," in *The Family Lifecycle,* ed. E. Carter and M. McGoldrick (New York: Gardner Press, 1980). See also E. H. Friedman, *Generation to Generation: Family Process in Church and Synagogue* (New York: Guilford Publications, 1980).

from what the rest of the world of family therapy, if not psychotherapy, appears to be aiming for, it should be given another name
completely.

Conclusion

The totally unexpected nature of the changes in my family and my thinking during the past generation has also led me to some thoughts about
future changes regarding Bowen theory and the family movement itself.
When I entered the field in 1968, in order to catch up I immediately pur-
chased all the back copies of *Family Process* (for almost $24), and for
another $75 secured all the well-known books published to that date —
but I will never be able to catch up again. Today the Bowen approach
is only one among many ways to understand families, and though it
may still be the only coherent system of family systems thinking yet
developed, it is little known, greatly misunderstood, often misquoted,
and referenced with terms long since discarded by its founder (e.g., ego-
mass). On the other hand, family of origin concepts are being applied
in inconceivably new directions, from cancer rehabilitation to organizational management, by people who were never trained at Georgetown,
know of Murray Bowen only as some prophet or folk hero, and have no
sense of his theory's biological and evolutionary imperative. They employ
the word "differentiation" synonymously with "individuation" or "autonomy." It well may be that the future significance of such concepts as
"multigenerational transmission," "emotional system," and "differentiation," if not all of Bowen theory — as well as any major contributions
to the evolution of these seminal ideas — will show up in political theory,
international relations, sports, economics — or even astronomy! Fantasy:
In the year 2150, one intergalactic research associate turns to another
and says, "You know, the other day I came across something on the origins of our parsec methods for spatial dichotomy, and according to the
notes, they were originally conceived in a field called family therapy."

Nine

MISCHIEF, MYSTERY, AND PARADOX
Bowen Theory and Therapy

It would be difficult to do justice to the depth and complexities of Bowen theory within the framework of an entire book, no less the confines of a single essay. This is so, in part, because many of its basic concepts are interdependent and require a constant circularity of exposition. It is also true because Bowen theory is really not about families per se, but about life. The task of explaining Bowen theory is something like being given the assignment, "Write a history of protoplasm in thirty pages." Rather than trying to "explain" it, therefore, this essay will be *about* it. I will focus on what I perceive to be the uniqueness of Bowen theory within the late-twentieth-century social and philosophical phenomenon that we have come to call "family therapy," and on what "the Bowen approach" has in common with pre-twenty-first-century thinking in other fields of scientific endeavor. Such a perspective may lead the reader to conclude that Bowen theory has more to do with cosmology, astronomy, or immunology than with "fixing" families, but, at the least, it will help differentiate differentiation. As both the family movement and his theory have evolved since Bowen published his first papers on the topic, "the Bowen approach" may now stand as more different from all other approaches to family therapy than family is itself different from individual model thinking. But those differences can serve as a framework for clarifying thinking.

First published as "Bowen Theory and Therapy," in *Handbook of Family Therapy*, vol. 2, ed. Alan S. Gurman and David P. Kniskern (Bristol, Pa.: Brunner/Mazel, 1991), 134–70.

One caveat is in order before proceeding, however. Precisely because Bowen theory is so tied up with the most fundamental issues of life, it is open to different understandings. What is about to be presented, therefore, is not meant to be the definitive view of Bowen theory. Rather, it is how one disciple who has spent two decades trying to apply it to families, institutions, and his own life has come to see it.

First, I will provide an overview of several characteristics of Bowen theory that set it apart from almost all other theories of family therapy. I will then discuss the theoretical significance for both his own theory and for the conceptualization of human life generally of four of Bowen's basic constructs, followed by an exposition of three principles that underlie the application of Bowen theory. As befits the Bowen approach, this essay will be weighted more in the direction of theory than practice, with discussion of practice serving to elucidate the theory further, rather than the theory being a prelude to learning technique. Finally, it will conclude with some thoughts designed to show that Bowen theory has the potential for being a true paradigm shift that challenges thinking in all the social sciences because of the way in which it reformats traditional dichotomies in the field, particularly with respect to culture, gender, pathology, and the process of healing.

Fundamental Characteristics of Bowen Theory

The Breadth of Its Perspective

As already stated, Bowen theory is not fundamentally about families, but about life. The fact that it can be applied to families is almost incidental to the wider focus that Bowen has tended to refer to as "the human phenomenon." But that wider focus extends beyond the human dimension to all of protoplasm, if not all of creation. Bowen has constantly emphasized over the years that we have more in common with other forms of protoplasm than differences, and that the traditional social science efforts to emphasize the differences, almost to the exclusion of the similarities, have decreased our objectivity about, and perhaps increased our denial of, what really makes us tick. Underpinning and infusing his ideas is the assumption that the human animal is part of evolutionary *emotional* processes that go back to the beginning of time, or at least to that propitious moment when the first eukaryotic cell (the first cell to develop a nucleus) appeared. It promptly separated itself from the hitherto only available process of reproduction (cloning), thus giving differentiation new meaning, and, possibly for the first time, giving rise to the existential, and perhaps biological, category of *self*. Therefore, what we observe in families today — the opposing forces for togetherness and self, the perpetual reactivity that undulates through any emotional system, the chronic anxiety that is transmitted from generation to generation, as well as the myriad of symptomatic labels that the social sciences have proliferated to describe these phenomena — are all a kind of background radiation that goes back to that "biological big bang." It is thus not really possible to comprehend the thrust of the Bowen approach to human families without also considering the nature of our entire species and its relationship to all existing life, and indeed to all previous life (and other natural systems) on this planet, if not throughout the cosmos.

In recent decades, for example, there has been an increased emphasis in academic papers on relating family life to other natural systems. Some are about other natural systems but do not make the explicit effort to relate them to human families. Previously the major application of Bowen theory was to a variety of family problems and families of origin; now we have papers by experts on whales, monkeys, ethology, sociobiology, slime molds, and so on. But, and this is crucial, *it is not simply comparisons of behavior that are being sought, but rather what is common to all "emotional," that is, natural, systems*. Similarly, in various parts of this essay, parallels will be shown between cellular processes and families. From a natural systems point of view, these comparisons may be seen as homologies rather than analogies. Analogies are comparisons; homologies are parallel evolutionary pathways. Bowen theory strongly suggests that humans, being colonies of cells, colonize like their cells. But if this is true, it is not because cells are the basic components to which humans can be reduced, but because humans develop the same kind of emotional fields (see especially Calhoun, 1963).

If it is characteristic of all family therapists to widen their focus from the individual to the family, then in Bowen's thinking, making the nuclear family the unit of observation is only a way station in that outward migration of perspective. Focus on the family is a way to maintain a direction that leads towards understanding the more encompassing natural systems that families mirror, and of which they are a part; that knowledge can then reciprocally help us to understand families. (Developing this evolutionary perspective is a large part of what "family of origin" work is about.) Bowen theory thus is very much a thinking therapist's therapy. That is not to say that it denies emotions — quite the contrary. The term "emotional" — as in "emotional system," "emotional triangle," or "emotional cutoff" — is constantly used in order to avoid a dichotomy between the psychological and the physical, and the emphasis on thinking is not to deny feeling but to emphasize the importance of self-regulation in the process of differentiation.

Bowen theory will always appeal more, however, to those therapists who tend to think in universals than to those whose primary concern is the immediacy of symptom relief. And the clients who seem to do best with it are those who both want to take responsibility for themselves and have the capacity to think beyond their own condition. The capacity to think about "the human phenomenon" from Bowen's natural systems perspective is itself an essential part of the therapeutic process. At the very least, the protoplasmic-cosmological context means that, on the one hand, all of life is germane to understanding families, and, on the other, the future of the human family is bound up with the evolution not only of our species, but of all life on this planet, and perhaps beyond. For the family therapist, as will be seen, this orientation leads to a "unified field theory" of family symptomatology and a connection between one's work with families and the ultimate course of one's own destiny. And, if ethologists are correct, then such commitment to the survival of one's species is also what we have in common with other forms of animal life. In this respect, Bowen's effort to apply his theory to the "human family" in his work on "societal regression" is a logical outcome of the breadth of his perspective.

A Perspective of Universals

A second major characteristic of Bowen's thinking that sets it apart from almost all other theories in the field is its tendency to conceptualize in terms of universal continua rather than discrete categories (e.g., nature/nurture, marital problems/child problems, male/female, patient/therapist, physical illness/emotional illness). Bowen theory constantly strives to make continuous what other theories dichotomize.

Encapsulated best in one of his favorite comments, "Schizophrenia is in all of us," its emphasis on the emotional forces common to all of protoplasm reduces the significance of the conventional divisions associated with culture, gender, pathology, and therapy, and changes radically what information a therapist should consider important. His concept that the family should be the "unit of observation (or treatment)," on the one hand, puts emphasis on the emotional forces common to all families, and, on the other, reduces greatly the significance of which family member bears the symptom.

From the other direction, the general tendency in the helping professions to catalogue existence according to traditional social science and psychiatric categories can throw people off regarding the understanding of Bowen theory. At various times, Bowen's ideas have been pigeonholed as behavioristic, holistic, biologically determined, learning theory, cognitive therapy, a throwback to psychoanalysis, or just plain cold — and, at times, Bowen theory will appear to belong less to therapy than to the disciplines of sociology, ethology, or anthropology. Actually, the natural systems aspect of Bowen theory suggests that dividing the subject matter of those three disciplines separately is artificial. Similarly, with regard to conventional divisions in psychiatry itself between, say, the humanistic (insight) and the biological (medicine), Bowen theory does not fit in one camp or the other. While it is rooted in biology and biological metaphor, the central Bowen concept of *differentiation* is about integrity, not the administration of drugs. Still another conventional dichotomy in the helping professions that can skew an understanding of Bowen theory is that between research and practice. As will be shown below, "re-search" is part and parcel of Bowen therapy.

Unless one understands that striving to comprehend the unity of life's forces is the intrinsic principle that gives all of Bowen theory its coherence, then viewing any particular aspect of the theory in isolation will give it the wrong slant. Thus, Bowen therapy is often thought of simplistically as the family of origin approach by those who are primarily concerned with technique. Ironically, systems thinking is all about understanding components in terms of their structures. It is vital not to confuse mode with melody. Many of Bowen's concepts will sound similar to ideas in other theories, and one can easily be misled about their meaning, unless they are heard within the creative matrix of his own central concepts, particularly natural systems and differentiation.

One important technical ramification of the theory's striving for unity, the way it streamlines the approaches to change, should also be mentioned in this context, and will be elaborated below. The unity of perspective turns the therapeutic endeavor of promoting differentiation into a broad-spectrum antibiotic that may be applied to any family no matter what its nature or the nature of its "dis-ease." For those who mistake complexity for depth, this may appear oversimplified, but streamlined formulations ($E=MC^2$, for example) also satisfy other time-honored criteria for the acceptance of a scientific theory, such as parsimony and aesthetic elegance.

According to Bowen, symptoms can show up in one of three locations: (1) in the marital relationship (as conflict, distance, or divorce); (2) in the health of one of the partners (physical or "mental"); or (3) in one of the children (though this last could also be placed in the space between parent and child). The same multigenerational forces create symptoms at any of these three locations. Bowen's concept that the family is the unit of observation (or treatment) means that what is important is not the location, or even the form, of the symptom that has surfaced at any of these sites, but getting to the systemic forces, both those within the nuclear family and those that are being transmitted from previous generations. An example of the power for different ways of thinking that Bowen theory offers is the different criterion that this focus on the nuclear family sets up for successful marriage. Instead of dividing marriages into two basic categories, those that last and those that do not, or those that are happy and those that are not, the new criterion based on the above model is that marriages are successful to the extent that the nuclear family is symptom-free in all three locations (with the understanding that no marriage achieves a grade better than 70 percent).

For a Bowen-trained therapist, therefore, the question of specialties ("Do you see couples? Individuals? Families with alcoholism, substance abuse, violence?") has no meaning. The "specialty" is always the same: skinning cats — in one way or another. This same focus on systemic emotional factors rather than specific problems or their location also applies to work systems, where differentiation in the leader becomes a more important goal than specific administrative solutions or improved managerial techniques, no matter what the type of organization. This leads to another continuity: family systems and work systems are both emotional systems.

There are two major ways in which this way of thinking is contrary to prevailing methods of conceptualization. The first is that it diminishes the importance of becoming expert in specific symptomatologies, or their location, as well as finding specific techniques for a broad array of issues; the second is that it is a principle that transcends culture. To appreciate how really different that is, it is only necessary to look through a year's supply of any family therapy (or other social science) journals, or to read the list of workshop topics at any helping-profession conference, and see that almost all of the presentations are on subject matter that Bowen theory says is irrelevant to understanding and modifying family process — not false, not inaccurate, but simply "not the information that counts." Similarly, most mental health programs and institutions organize themselves around foci that Bowen theory says should be defocused.

One small example that will serve both to illustrate and to metaphorize how Bowen theory constantly comes in at a tangent to accepted dichotomies in the field is his view of what is essential in the functioning of the human brain. Most discussion of the brain in psychological circles today splits it longitudinally by hemispheres, "right brain" and "left brain," and there is much emphasis on their separate functions, as well as on the categorizing of people in terms of which hemisphere seems to be more influential in their mental processes. The brain division that Bowen has emphasized, however, is on a horizontal plane. Using McLean's theories of "the triune brain" (McLean, 1985), Bowen theory sees the right-brain/left-brain distinctions as subsets of the far more crucial distinction between the cortex and the limbic system. The view is that a person's *method* of perceiving, conceptualizing, or expressing ideas is far less significant than, and is always a function of, a more continuous fundamental process: one's ability to regulate one's reactivity, that is, differentiation.

The Emotional Being of the Therapist

A third characteristic of the Bowen approach that distinguishes it from other family theories is its emphasis on the self-development of the therapist. Bowen has consistently maintained that it is hard for the patient to mature beyond the maturity level of the therapist, no matter how good his or her technique. In Bowen theory, the *differentiation of the therapist is technique.* As will be seen below, the capacity of a therapist to apply Bowen theory is a function of the therapist's own differentiation. According to Bowen theory, therefore, maintaining a nonanxious presence, or being objective, or even promoting differentiation in others, is connected to the *being* of the therapist, not to his or her know-how. Here, Bowen theory again makes continuous what other theories would categorize separately, that is, the distinction between a therapist's supervision and his or her own "therapy," as an essential part of training in the Bowen school involves the therapist's working on his or her own differentiation. From the point of view of a Bowen-trained supervisor, the therapist can bring in situations either from client families or from his or her own family of origin. Indeed, if the differentiation of the therapist *is* technique, bringing cases of *other* families to one's supervisor may not even be the optimal way to receive supervision. (The extent to which this idea can be viewed as radical in some quarters is evidenced by the fact that Bowen-trained therapists have sometimes had difficulty receiving certification from some professional accreditation boards on the grounds that seeing the same person for supervision and therapy is unethical or unhealthy.)

There is another, perhaps more essential way in which "the being of the therapist" is related to the functioning or at least the thinking of the therapist in Bowen theory. Kerr (1981) has stated that it may not be possible to comprehend Bowen theory merely by reading about it or attending workshops. He has suggested that the therapist must first go through an emotional change. While such a notion smacks of cultism and "true believers" and can lead to the dangerous *ad hominem* position that if you disagree with the concepts, you are not differentiated (how do you distinguish those who disagree from those who cannot hear it?), to the extent that Kerr's observation is accurate, then Bowen theory may belong to that method of inquiry that can be learned only by apprenticing to the master or the master's disciples. While to some that characteristic may be enough to invalidate such thinking as more befitting the occult, the master-disciple relationship has always been an acceptable method of passing on a learned tradition in our civilization, sometimes with spectacular results. It is not possible, for example, to understand the Talmud simply by reading translations, or even a book on how the talmudists reasoned, or the meaning of their technical terms and pet phrases. One must study for some time with those who know the process. Similarly, a thorough grasp of Bowen theory is probably achievable only by studying the concepts over some period in the context of encountering one's own experience of life while maintaining some type of disciple relationship with someone who has already gone through the process. For those who might consider such teaching processes as more befitting religion than science, it should be noted that there exists evidence that Nobel prize winners in the hard sciences have frequently been part of multigenerational traditions of teachers who were Nobel laureates (Zuckerman, 1967), suggesting, among other things, that a successful way of thinking had been passed down through apprenticeship.

To the extent that Kerr's comment is accurate, the notion that an emotional change is as crucial to the training process as to the treatment process is unique to Bowen theory among family therapies, and it has a curious parallel in its application. That parallel has to do with patients who do everything "right" according to Bowen's prescriptions and still do not make progress. They, too, must first go through some emotional change analogous to what the therapist had experienced in his or her training before *their* "technique" will work — and if the therapist did not experience that shift, the client is not likely to do so.

Four Seminal Constructs

What follows are four major interlocking concepts in Bowen theory that underpin all of Bowen's other ideas and that "differentiate" Bowen theory from other family theories. As stated earlier, they will be presented not to explain them, but to show their theoretical significance both for the theory itself and for theorizing about families generally. Those constructs are *differentiation, emotional system, multigenerational transmission,* and *emotional triangles.* In the original formulation of his theory, Bowen referred to eight basic concepts. The other four are *nuclear family, family projection process, sibling position* (see also Toman, 1961), and *societal regression.* In addition, he later began to add,

but never finished developing, a ninth, *spirituality*. Because of space limitations, only four have been selected for discussion here — those deemed
to best elucidate the thrust of this essay, the uniqueness of Bowen theory.
The others are referred to in passing, and *societal regression* is discussed
specifically in the conclusion. A fuller explanation of all of them can be
found in Kerr (1981) or Bowen (1978).

Bowen's major constructs are interdependent. None is fully under-
standable without some comprehension of the other three, and all are
held together by a premise that subsumes the entire theory, that there is
a *chronic anxiety* in all of life that comes with the territory of living. It
may manifest itself differently in different species, families, or cultures,
and different families will vary in the intensity of chronic anxiety they
exhibit, depending on such other variables as basic levels of differentiation and the position a given nuclear unit occupies on their own extended
family tree, but it is essentially the same phenomenon.

What Bowen refers to as "chronic anxiety" is not to be confused with
worries about a specific problem of living, nor is it reducible to a pho-
bia or a compulsion. "Chronic anxiety" is a far more pervasive, natural
systems phenomenon of which the specific foci of personal anxiety are
only the tracers. In psychoanalytic theory, anxiety is distinguished from
fear as being a fear that is unfounded. Bowen's concept of chronic anxiety includes that notion, but a natural systems context suggests it is less
something that is unnatural (that is, neurotic) than the exaggeration of
a basic rhythm of life: the instinctual, nonthinking response necessary
for wilderness survival as well as the habits required for playing sports.
At times, the role of chronic anxiety in Bowen theory may seem to have
something in common with the part played by *angst* in existential philosophical systems, but Bowen has taught it less as a quality of the human
mind than as a biological phenomenon that humans have in common
with all forms of life. Sometimes chronic anxiety appears to play the
same theoretical role as Freud's *libido,* an energizing force. It cannot be
equated with angst or libido, however, and must be considered in terms
that are universal to all creatures on this planet.

For Bowen, chronic anxiety is the emotional and physical reactivity
shared by all protoplasm, the responses that are automatic rather than
mediated by the cortex. It is transmitted from previous generations by
families both cumulatively and idiosyncratically, and it is experienced

and expressed more intensely by various individual members of our species because of the way previous generations in their families have channeled the transmission of their own. But the transmission does not begin with our own families; it is a natural systems phenomenon that goes back to the beginning of life on this planet (in this universe?). "Aha," you say, "but lower forms of life do not have a cortex, so the comparison is of apples and oranges."

That is just the point. The cortex is not always as dominant as *Homo sapiens* would like to believe. When our anxiety is low, our unencumbered thought processes enable us to differentiate from other forms of life, from previous generations, and from one another, but when our anxiety is high, what we think is thinking is merely mental activity. Cerebration also can be reactivity, that is, in the service of chronic anxiety, and you can be as reactive with your left brain as with your right. Another way of putting this is to say that cerebration can be considered thinking, according to Bowen theory, only when it is in the service of, or is the result of, differentiating processes. Thus, clearheadedness (and therefore differentiation), while solely a human attribute, is achievable only by dealing with the same emotional forces that affect all other species. It is this connection between our emotional beings and the functioning of our cortex that leads to the study of all forms of colonized life. And, as we will see below regarding Bowen therapy, the omnipresence of chronic anxiety in all human systems lays the groundwork for striving for objectivity in the functioning of any Bowen-trained therapist. In all events, *chronic anxiety is understood to be the primary promoter of all symptoms, from schizophrenia to cancer, from anorexia to birth defects. The antidote, and the preventive medicine, is always differentiation.*

Differentiation

Differentiation is the lifelong process of striving to keep one's being in balance through the reciprocal external and internal processes of self-definition and self-regulation. It is a concept that sometimes can be difficult to focus on objectively. As the emotional system of family therapists has evolved over the past quarter-century, the term has almost become a buzzword that identifies its user as a follower of Bowen. No one trained in any other major family therapy school would ever use the word anymore, even in passing, lest he or she be defined as belonging to the wrong school. For their part, of course, Bowen's disciples never use the term "enmeshed" (a buzzword of the "structuralists") to imply the opposite of differentiation, which they call "fusion." Ironically, a term that was coined in the service of objectivity has become emotion-laden and a source of much reactivity. Nothing, of course, shows less differentiation, since *differentiation* means the capacity to become oneself out of one's self with minimum reactivity to the positions or reactivity of others. Differentiation is charting one's own way by means of one's own internal guidance system, rather than perpetually eyeing the "scope" to see where others are.

Differentiation as used by Bowen refers more to a process than to a goal that can ever be achieved. (When people say, "I differentiated from my wife, my child, my parent, etc.," that proves they do not understand the concept.) It refers to a direction in life rather than a state of being, to the capacity to take a stand in an intense emotional system, to saying "I" when others are demanding "we," to containing one's reactivity to the reactivity of others (which includes the ability to avoid being polarized), to maintaining a nonanxious presence in the face of anxious others. It refers, as well, to knowing where one ends and another begins, to being able to cease automatically being one of the system's emotional dominoes, to being clear about one's own personal values and goals, to taking maximum responsibility for one's own emotional being and destiny rather than blaming others or the context: culture, gender, or environmental forces. It is an emotional concept, not a cerebral one, but it does require clearheadedness. And it has enormous consequence for new ways of thinking about leadership. But it is, as Bowen liked to say, a lifetime project, with no one ever getting more than 70 percent of the way to the goal.

Differentiation is not to be equated, however, with similar-sounding ideas such as individuation, autonomy, or independence. First of all, it has less to do with a person's behavior than, as mentioned, with his or her emotional being. Second, there is a sense of connectedness to the concept that prevents the mere gaining of distance or leaving, no less cutting off, from being the way to achieve it. Third, as stated above, it has to do with the fabric of one's existence, one's integrity. Obviously, differentiation has its origin in the biological notion that cells can have no identity, purpose, or distinctiveness until they have separated from —

that is, left — their progenitors (differentiation is a prerequisite to specialization even if one is ultimately going to fuse to accomplish one's purpose). But also implicit in this biological metaphor or homologue is the idea that such a self has little meaning if the cell cannot connect. In its simplest terms, therefore, differentiation is the capacity to be one's own integrated aggregate-of-cells person while still belonging to, or being able to relate to, a larger colony.

Such a biological metaphor also has ramifications for thinking and the conduct of therapy, since the incapacity to achieve some balance in the self–togetherness struggle will tend to create a style of thinking that shows up in either/or, all-or-nothing, black-and-white conceptualizations and, eventually, family cutoffs. Conversely, the capacity to think systemically and avoid the polarizations characteristic of reactivity seems to go along with the emotional growth associated with differentiation. The major theoretical significance of differentiation for the overall development of Bowen theory, and for theorizing in the social sciences generally, is as follows: A problem common to all social science theorizing is that the more accurately any system of thought can make predictions, the less room it allows for free will. It is one thing to develop a theory about subatomic particles, plate tectonics, or black holes and, without any conflict at all, use as a criterion of the theory's validity its power for prediction. When the subject matter is the human animal, however, then the more elegant the theory, the less dignity is left for the human. It is, after all, precisely because the human is not a soulless star or particle that social science theory always fails to gain the same measure of certainty found in the "hard" sciences. It may be the awareness of this dilemma that has led many family therapists to try to synthesize family and individual model thinking.

Bowen's way of handling the problem has been to develop his systems theory consistent with natural systemic concepts despite the uncontrollable or unknowable implicit in the human animal having animus, but to leave room for a variable that could account for the differences, the inconsistencies, and the otherwise unexplainables that result from human will. What Bowen's concept of differentiation does is to supply a variable that allows the rest of the theory to be developed in a systematic, consistent manner. But it keeps the theory honest by allowing for exceptions. In addition, the variable provided by differentiation helps Bowen theory deal with a problem common to all systems theory: how to account for change at all if systems are perpetually kept in balance by their own homeostatic forces. Why, for example, do some identified patients improve despite the system, or why, despite the impeccable logic of systemic thinking, do things sometimes just not turn out the way they are supposed to? And why do the elements that we assume have caused pathology in one system not have pathogenic effects in another?

It is perhaps in this context that Bowen's scale of differentiation (Kerr, 1981) can best be understood. The scale is an effort to say that despite the universality of systems concepts, people are different. But, the scale suggests, the differences that count are not to be found in the categories of information that are traditional sociological classifications, nor can those differences be understood in the conventions of psychodynamics. What counts, according to the scale, is a person's capacity to function in a differentiated manner, as that term was defined above. And that is more a function of sibling position, triangles, and multigenerational processes than of gender, culture, or environmental conditioning.

Bowen's scale of differentiation is connected to Bowen theory's striving for unity. It is a lens for looking at the breadth of humanity in a manner that is continuous, not an effort to create a Brave New World of "alpha pluses" and "delta minuses." When Bowen first published his "scale," he was astounded to see how many missed the significance of continuity and began to use the scale against itself by employing it in their research to create discrete categories. That is precisely not what the scale is about.

Carried to its logical conclusion, the scale has problems. For example, if you were to reach 100 on the scale, would you have all friends (since you could presumably then relate to anybody) or no friends, since at 100 who could relate to you? On the other hand, Liebnitz's theory of limits in calculus also breaks down at infinity. The usefulness of a theoretical concept is not necessarily destroyed by inconsistencies within it. What counts is its *power* to engender new thinking and glean observations that other models do not permit.

One way of demonstrating the power of Bowen's scale of differentiation to create a different perspective is with the accompanying diagram. Here the horizontal axis, marked "condition," is the intensity of the

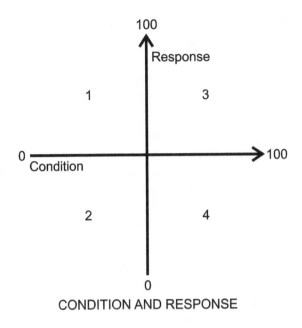

CONDITION AND RESPONSE

family symptom, crisis, or anxiety attendant upon the crisis. The vertical axis, labeled "response," is the degree of differentiation in a person or a family, and is always inversely proportional to the amount of chronic anxiety transmitted to the system from previous generations. If you were to plot families or individuals along both axes, you would find that they would distribute themselves in all four quadrants. Those in quadrant 1 would not be likely to become dysfunctional, either because, objectively, they were not in crisis (scoring low on the horizontal scale), or because the crises that they were experiencing were not overwhelming since their level of differentiation (their position on the vertical scale) was high. Those in quadrant 2 also score low in the objective intensity of their crises (the horizontal scale), but more of them will develop symptoms because their level of differentiation (their capacity to deal with the crises they do experience) is also low on the vertical scale. In other words, such families may be lucky and not experience many critical events, but when they do, those crises will be magnified by their low level of differentiation. It will simply take less to throw them. Because, however, the normal tendency is to chart our existential position in life only on the horizontal scale (leaving out the differentiation variable), families in this quadrant (and often their therapists) will perceive themselves (unobjectively) to be further along the horizontal axis than they actually are.

This is brought sharply into relief by the fact that families in quadrant 3 are actually experiencing a higher degree of crises (horizontal scale), but because they are less reactive and handle their crises better (also high on the differentiation scale), they will, owing to the relative lack of symptoms, appear to be lower on the horizontal scale than they are. They are also less stressed because they handle their stress better. Again, however, by observing these families from a single-pole perspective, one might assume that they simply have fewer problems. It would be more accurate to say that these families have a greater likelihood of recuperation because their degree of resiliency of response is high. Also implicit here is the notion that symptoms have more to do with a family's position on the vertical axis than on the horizontal axis. In other words, symptoms are less related to strain (external pressure) than to stress (response). Thinking about stress as a vertical-axis phenomenon rather than a horizontal "condition" has, of course, major ramifications for taking responsibility for stress, as the term is normally used.

By contrast, the families most likely to dysfunction are those in quadrant 4, who score high on the horizontal scale and low on the vertical scale of differentiation, which, after all, really concerns their capacity to handle life's problems. They are the families least likely to heal. From a single-variable point of view, they will be viewed as dysfunctional simply because of the objective nature of their condition (disease, environment, existential dilemmas, family crises, etc.), whereas the bipolar perspective enables one to see that with the same amount of objective crisis (condition) in their lives, they still might have been less dysfunctional had their level of differentiation placed them in quadrant 3.

The most useful way to express the relationship between condition and response illustrated by this bipolar graph is as follows (keeping in mind that the differentiation level has a great deal to do with the amount of chronic anxiety transmitted from previous generations): given the same objective circumstances, families or individuals are more likely to dysfunction or develop symptoms *to the extent that* their differentiation is low, and to tolerate more intense symptoms, or rebound better from intense crises, *to the extent that* their differentiation is high. The bipolar graph also illustrates Bowen's methods of conceptualization because it emphasizes continuity rather than discrete categories. (Graphs make things more "graphic" than is true about any spectrum of humanity.) As stated above, the very capacity to think in terms of "to the extent that" rather than "either/or" is essential to Bowen theory conceptualization.

Finally, there is one clinical aspect of the concept of differentiation that should be highlighted here because it also helps illustrate how different Bowen theory can be. The concept of differentiation is a focus on strength rather than pathology. It comes up fully on the side of personal responsibility rather than faulting the stars, society, the environment, or one's parents, for that matter. Despite the tinge of predestination associated with multigenerational transmission, differentiation is inherently an antivictim, antiblaming focus. Just as it is a variable that prevents systemic concepts from "blowing away" individual dignity, so too, when it comes to change, precisely because differentiation is a focus on the individual's response, it refuses to allow the system to take all the responsibility. And that is why, as will be seen below, Bowen therapy focuses on the vertical axis for both client and therapist.

The Emotional System

A second basic construct in Bowen theory is the concept of an emotional system. It is interdependent with the aforementioned concept of differentiation and the concept of multigenerational transmission (to be explored next). It is, in fact, the context that joins them.

The term "emotional system" refers to any group of people or other colonized forms of protoplasm (herds, flocks, troops, packs, schools, swarms, and aggregates) that have developed emotional interdependencies to the point where the resulting system through which the parts are connected (administratively, physically, or emotionally) has evolved its own principles of organization. The structure, or resulting field, therefore, tends to influence the functioning of the various members more than any of the components tend to influence the functioning of the system. A family emotional system includes the members' thoughts, feelings, emotions, fantasies, associations, and past connections, individually and together. It includes their physical makeup, genetic heritage, and current metabolic states. It involves their sibling position and their parents' sibling positions. It rotates on the axes of their respective paths within the multigenerational processes transmitted from their own families of origin, including the fusion and the cutoffs. It includes the emotional history of the system itself, particularly the conditions under which it originally took shape; the effect upon it of larger emotional and physical forces; how it has dealt with transitions, particularly loss; and the quality of differentiation in the system, both now and in the past, particularly of those at the top. In effect, it includes all the information that can be put on a family's genogram.

Bowen has come to use the term "family" as synonymous with "emotional system," so defined. An emotional system is not to be equated, however, with a "relationship system" or a "communication system," though it includes them. In fact, Bowen has gone out of his way to avoid the terminology of information theory, general systems theory, or cybernetics when describing an "emotional system," because "self" from a natural systems' point of view is not a concept; it is a dynamic reality capable of maturation. Cybernetics is for cyborgs. It is also Bowen theory's rootedness in the evolutionary processes of all natural systems that makes the concept of an emotional system equally valid for an organ or an organization.

There are two aspects of Bowen's concept of a family as an emotional system that help bring out the distinctiveness of Bowen theory. One is the criterion that this concept establishes for what information is important; the second is how this method of conceptualization is similar to the antireductionist, field-theory models emerging in other scientific disciplines.

Regarding criteria for information, family therapy currently is in an informational bind. Every family will produce an encyclopedia of information about itself. Is the therapist simply to write down dutifully every fact he or she hears? Not only is that impossible, but such a focus on the content of what is heard is likely to fuse ("enmesh") the therapist in the emotional processes of the family. Many facts reported by family members, particularly cultural and environmental explanations for their functioning, while appearing to be helpful, often are really efforts to deny personal responsibility or to obfuscate emotional process. Objective observation is eroded if the therapist is trying to observe everything. The problem of data gathering is intensified by the fact that every therapist today regularly receives notices of books or conferences on literally hundreds of symptoms and new approaches. Since information generally increases at an exponential rate, the problem can only get worse. One can never catch up. Not only is it impossible in such an atmosphere to be objective, but to the extent that members of the helping professions moor their sense of confidence in their knowledge of pathology or technique, they are doomed always to feeling inadequate. The way out of this bind is not to specialize, which only sends the avalanche of information in the opposite direction, but to find criteria for what information is important.

This is precisely the function of Bowen's concept of an emotional system. It concentrates the focus of what to take note of (primarily, levels of differentiation, interlocking triangles, and chronic anxiety), and it reduces greatly the importance of the data that many other approaches to family therapy consider significant, if not vital, by seeing such information as the content rather than the driving force of emotional process. For example, from the perspective of an emotional system, culture does not "cause" family process. It stains it (that is, makes it visible). Culture, rather than being the formative process, is the medium through which family process works its art. Elsewhere (Friedman, 1985) I have tried to show that, using Bowen theory, it is possible to develop laws of family process regarding such factors as loss replacement, cutoffs, pain thresholds, the similarity of opposite extremes, secrets, triangles, chronic conditions, and the like that have the same relevance for all families irrespective of culture. And to the extent that there is divergence between two families with respect to these laws, those differences cannot be traced back to cultural, environmental, or gender differences, but to factors that involve levels of chronic anxiety and differentiation.

Another way of putting this is as follows: The concept of an emotional system suggests that if you knew all of the cultural and environmental factors in a family's background, but knew nothing about the family members' emotional processes as defined by Bowen theory, you could not make very accurate predictions about how they will fare in the future. On the other hand, if you knew all the emotional process factors as defined by Bowen theory, you would not need to know any of the background cultural factors in order to make very accurate predictions about that family's future. From the perspective of an emotional system, cultural and environmental factors are far less important than is the timing of significant changes; the kind of people they are (their personalities) and their backgrounds are less important than the positions they occupy in the triangles of their contemporary systems and the paths of multigenerational transmission.

The second aspect of the emotional system concept that helps sharpen the distinctiveness of Bowen theory is its similarity to what has come to be called *field theory* in other sciences (Sheldrake, 1988), particularly physics, astronomy, and biology. In recent years, within all of these areas of inquiry there has been some movement away from the notion that structures can be understood in terms of their components (matter) alone. In physics, together with the tradition of progressively narrowing the focus to smaller and smaller particles in an effort to try to find the elementary components of matter (from atom — which means uncuttable — to electron to lepton to quark), another approach has been developing that defocuses that infinitely regressive search. It tries to understand all matter not as particles, but as waves in a *field*. One of the reasons for going in this direction, besides the bottomless pit found in the search for elementary particles, is a striving for unity, an effort to understand the four major forces of the universe with one theory. Parallel thinking has gone on in astronomy with models called *string theory* that suggest that matter and energy are laid out across the heavens in patterns established by the original big bang and function dynamically in patterns that are still evolving from (and therefore are still in touch with) those initiating events.

In biology, a similar effort to get away from explaining protoplasm purely in terms of genetic programs has received new impetus. There has always been some awareness that certain biological phenomena are not explainable, and, indeed, seem to go against, the notion of genetic determinism alone, but the new technologies of microbiology have provided more evidence for the fact that genes no more may be the basic constituents of protoplasm than atoms are the basic constituents of matter (Webster & Goodwin, 1982). Actually, from this perspective, what has been given up is the importance of the notion of basic constituents. For what is now realized in both physics and biology is that the way constituent particles function is not necessarily according to their own nature alone, but often is due to their position within force fields that encompass them. In other words, change their position and they will function differently; change the forces and they will appear to have different natures. Genes, for example, can function differently depending on their position on a chromosome. The rotation of the axis of symmetry of an amphibious embryo can result in its producing twins. The transplantation of cells to another location on a chick embryo can result in the cells developing partly according to their nature and partly according to their position on the embryo. One can cut away parts of certain embryos in an early-enough stage and they will still produce a complete creature, though smaller. Here is a description in terms of field theory of the relationship of Jupiter and her moons that might just as easily be a description of schizophrenia within the relationship system of a family:

> Gases from Jupiter's moons are transported to Jupiter by the magnetic field between them, thus providing atmosphere to their host's planet — it is reasonable to consider the field as the operative entity, with planet and satellites as nodes within it.

What the Bowen concept of an emotional system has in common with field theory in biology and physics is, first of all, a striving for the unity of all forces; second, a veering away from materialistic reductionism (explaining structures in terms of their components); and third, an emphasis, instead, on the forces in the field and the position of various members within the field (thus, the emphasis on triangles, multigenerational transmission, sibling position, and "I" position). Indeed, Bowen has, at times, used the phrase "emotional field" rather than emotional system. So used, a field may be defined as an environment of influence that is not material in itself (a magnetic or gravitational field, for example), but comes into existence because of the proximity of matter to matter. However, once the field does come into being, it has more power to influence the discrete particles within it than any of those pieces of matter can continue to influence the field they have, by their presence, "caused" to exist.

Bowen's emphasis on emotional rather than environmental or cultural factors can be understood as an effort to stay focused on the field. And *differentiation*, within this context, becomes making oneself aware of the encompassing fields, as well as one's position in them, so that one can make choices.

One application of the concept of emotional systems that will help illustrate field theory is an approach to leadership I have been calling "leadership through self-differentiation" (Friedman, 1985). Early in my experience as a supervisor, I noticed that whenever a member of the helping professions was having difficulty functioning creatively, imaginatively, or in a well-defined manner in any institution (hospital, clinic, or partnership), the person leading his or her organization was poorly defined: a person who rarely took stands, a peace-monger, someone without vision, someone who was more a reactor than an initiator. Later, I learned that this was true for all organizations — military, religious, educational, business, and familial.

As a result, in supervising leaders of any kind of institution, including the family, I have taught that if the person at the top will focus primarily on his or her own differentiation (i.e., providing vision, defining self, working at being a nonanxious presence, while taking care to remain connected), then such functioning will have a systemic effect on the rest of the individuals in the organization, that is, the organizational field. (Often a person who can do this will tend to become the one "at the top" even if he or she does not have the title.) When the "head" of any institution moves in a better differentiated direction, not only will everyone become more productive, but their relationships with one another also will improve. What distinguishes this notion of leadership as a field theory concept is that it is not saying that the leader (or parent) becomes a model to emulate. Rather than serving as a primary copy to be replicated, what leadership through self-differentiation affects is the field, which then affects the components within it. It is not a matter of specific behavior by a leader leading to similar specific behavior by a follower. Direct connection or observation between the head and the other components around specific issues is not involved. The components are not influenced because they learn to do by observing or through "identification." Leadership through self-differentiation is based on an organic concept: it is the nature of organic fields (the human body or a body politic) that when one of the components (an organ or an organism) can evolve to the position of "head" and then differentiate itself, the systemic ramification of that connectedness through the entire emotional system (field) is what influences the functioning of the other components and the nature of their relationships with one another.

Other evidence for the field theory aspect of this process is that when leaders (heads), or parents, can be taught to function in this way, chronic ailments in the system that appear to be unconnected often seem to go quietly away, though usually no clear cause-and-effect chain is visible. And the principle seems to transcend the size of the following. The head of an elephant, after all, has as much influence on its body as does the head of a chinchilla on its body. The process seems similar to the uncanny self-regulation processes found in successful biofeedback where, through information loops, thinking can change cellular and, hitherto considered involuntary, glandular responses. It is also similar to any situation in which a person suffers from a variety of chronic conditions for which there are a myriad of appropriate specialists, and then finds that a change in central metabolic processes, and sometimes in his or her vision about life's goals, affects all symptoms at once.

Finally, it should be mentioned here that Bowen's emotional systems or field concept produces one more example of continuity where there has traditionally been dichotomy. Through the basicness of its biological metaphor, the concept of an emotional system breaks down the usual distinctions among different types of institutional life (sports, business, health care, religion, etc.) and unifies that which promotes the health of institutions with that which promotes personal physical well-being. All this, in turn, feeds back to the notion mentioned above that in Bowen theory, thinking is an emotional phenomenon — and so, then, also must be leadership. If that is so, then management consultants will have no more luck changing corporations or partnerships fundamentally than therapists are able to bring essential change to families as long as they focus on technical, managerial, and administrative solutions rather than on promoting differentiation (an emotional change) at the top.

Multigenerational Transmission

Of all Bowen's central concepts, it may be the multigenerational perspective that gives the others their distinctiveness. At first, the concept sounds similar to what all social science research would accept: that the past influences the present. There is a difference, however. For Bowen, it is not simply the influence of the past, but it is, to use Rupert Sheldrake's phrase, "the presence of the past." Basically, the concept states that emotional responses, both their nature and the degree of their intensity, are passed down from "generation to generation," a triple entendre that means not only (1) parents to children, but also (2) the replication from any consecutive stages of reproduction, and (3) the overall process itself. Such transmission is conducted through all the conduits of an emotional system as defined above. In addition, while families differ in the way they do this, differences between families have less to do with cultural or environmental characteristics of the family (which, as stated, supply the medium of expression rather than the driving process) than with the position of those families as weak or strong limbs on their larger extended family tree, and, ultimately, the position of those extended families as limbs on the human family tree. What most defines where any nuclear family grouping (or any member within a family) is situated on those trees is the basic level of chronic anxiety or its reciprocal, the basic level of differentiation of self, that multigenerational processes have formatted and reinforced over the generations. The same phenomenon seems to apply to "branches" of an organization.

More is involved here, however, than the *conditioning* of the past, or something we have inherited or *introjected* from our ancestors. Bowen's multigenerational transmission concept is rooted in the notion that all generations are part of a *continuous natural process,* with each generation pressing up against the next, so that past and present almost become a false dichotomy. (Even with "time," Bowen theory makes continuous what is conventionally categorized separately.) It is this warping of time, so to speak, that gives Bowen's theory of transmission its special dimension and differentiates it from other theories that emphasize the "influence" of the past. Not only does it suggest you "can go home again," the intimation is that you never left.

As mystical as this sounds, it has some extraordinary similarities to the aforementioned effort to understand the cosmos known as *string theory.* (The fact that you tear off a page from the calendar does not mean that that unit of time has actually ceased to exist.) Thus, not only can the future be predicted on the basis of the past, but the past can be reconstructed on the basis of the ever-evolving present.

"Working on one's family of origin," therefore, as the phrase has come to be used, is far more than a matter of scaring up one's ancestors like Gilbert and Sullivan's *Duke of Rudigore.* And it is even more than learning to "understand" one's parents or to reconnect with theirs. The connection that is important is with the natural processes that are formatting one's destiny, processes that not only go back for generations, but ultimately to all life's processes since creation. The specifics, therefore, of researching cutoffs; finding long-lost relatives; correlating dates of change; delineating interlocking triangles; noting similarities of symptoms, issues, and the positions of those who become symptomatic over the generations; or changing one's responses to habitual family interactions, while useful in their own right for obtaining distance from, and (one would hope) gaining more objectivity about, one's present emotional state, have a far more fundamental purpose. *They are angles of entry into the universal, if not cosmic, processes that have formed our being.* It is the capacity to get in touch with that process, to know it and experience it, to be affected by it all over again, and then not to be reactive to it, that, according to Bowen theory, is the source of self-differentiation. And, says Bowen theory, to the extent that individuals can accomplish that, they will find an immediate carryover to functioning in all their relationships. It is here that we can see the *raison d'être* for family of origin focus as a form of supervision of therapists. Not only does it increase self-differentiation, an essential factor in dealing with anxiety, but it also gives the therapist firsthand "familiarity" with the basic life processes — which, according to Bowen theory, are what we are really dealing with anyway, no matter what the family problem.

Bowen first became aware of the latter ramifications of the multigenerational transmission process while working with medical residents. He noticed that they became better physicians when, in the course of their working on their own marriages, they were induced to go back to their families of origin. In recent years, I have had a similar experience with members of the clergy. Every minister, no matter what his or her denomination, who has come in for help with a crisis in faith has found that the crisis atrophied when he or she used the conflict as an entree back into the emotional processes of his or her family of origin. In other words, their religious commitment became clearer and more self-affirmed when the ministers came into contact with, and were able to differentiate themselves from, the same emotional processes that contributed to their originally joining the clergy. Such increased differentiation has almost never led to their leaving their profession. What happens seems more akin to their acquiring it for their own.

The significance of Bowen's multigenerational transmission concept for his own theory is, as already stated, that it puts the entire theory into the framework of natural systems, that is, life in this cosmos. The significance for family therapy, and theory generally, is its deemphasis on symptoms in the process of obtaining change, and the setting of different criteria for judging the severity of a problem. In ascertaining the degree of illness in a given family tree, it focuses more on the structure of the root system than on the immediate fruitfulness or barrenness of its boughs.

One clinical example will illustrate this. A therapist has two families come in who are in apparently similar situations. In both, say, there are anorexic girls of about the same age, from similar socioeconomic backgrounds, and with similar sibling positions, similar weights, similar petulance, similar conflicts of will with their parents, a similar degree of anxiety in their parents about the symptom, and so on. Family diagrams, however, show that in one system there is evidence everywhere of failure to cope: early death, lack of reproduction, a great deal of divorce and marital conflict, other members of the patient's generation (cousins) often focused or dysfunctional. In the genogram of the other girl, however, the evidence everywhere is of strength and resiliency. On the basis of that multigenerational comparison, one can make a far better prediction of which child has the better chance of recuperation than one could based on information about the present state of things.

The most significant ramification of the way in which multigenerational transmission deemphasizes the focus on specific symptomatology is as follows. Much, if not most, of the change that occurs in families and other institutions does not last. And much of what we thought was change often recycles either in a different form or in a different location. Much change is merely transformation. In true change, something remains the same. The illusions of change and the recycling of symptoms are attributable to what may be called "the myth of the primary site," which is the assumption that disease or dysfunction originates in the place in which it first surfaces or to which it can be traced back. The alternative to that way of thinking, however, is not to say that it began in a different location, but to assume that what is *primary* is not a site but the coming together of necessary and sufficient processes at a particular moment. In other words, the onset is not caused by something natural to the specific *location* where it "began," but by the fact that it was at a propitious moment in a multigenerational emotional transmission process. Bowen has analogized this process to a tornado that can only come into being when all the right conditions of temperature, pressure, and humidity are met simultaneously. If only two are satisfied, you do not get two-thirds of a tornado. He has applied this way of thinking to physical illness, for example, suggesting that both emotional and physical conditions must be satisfied simultaneously. However, it can really be applied to the formation of any symptom or dysfunction in a person, a family, or an organization.

Problem-afflicted churches and synagogues illustrate the primary-site paradox well, though it can be found in all institutions to the extent that they become involved in the family process. Every religious hierarchy has institutions that are known as "pills" or as "plums," and the members of the clergy in any denomination know well which they are. The plums tend to have three clergy in a century; the pills tend to spit them out every other year, if not twice a year. The failures of all hierarchies, no matter what the denomination, to change these institutions are identical, and their overall batting average is about the same as that in the war on cancer. The usual response is to put in new, better, healthier, younger clergy. But as with cancer, malignant processes are not changed by "new blood." Similarly, the clergy in congregations that tend to the pill end of the spectrum often become engaged in long, bitter battles to get rid of a few dissidents; sometimes they are successful, but often, even after such excision, they find the problem resurfacing several years later in "cells" that had never had contact with the "cells" that left. It is as when a surgeon says, "We found a small malignancy, but don't worry, we got it all." "Getting it all" assumes that the disease process *began* in the primary site. Still another way of asking the question that will show we are always dealing with processes rather than location or specific amounts of matter is: Where does something go when it is said to have gone into remission?

Not only does Bowen's concept of the multigenerational transmission process avoid the will-o'-the-wisp of the primary site, but it also offers new ways for understanding institutional character. Again, using churches and synagogues as models for any institution, one might begin by asking what was present in their early development that allows some to recuperate faster or with less trauma. It is not that they do not face the same issues. Many religious institutions are thrown off track when the separation (divorce) from some minister was poorly handled. The origins of many "pills" begin in a split from another congregational colony. Still another possibility worth researching is that all institutions "institutionalize" the emotional processes (and the pathology) of the founding families. Since law firms, professional sports teams, businesses, professional partnerships, and many healthcare institutions replicate similar phenomena, Bowen's concept of multigenerational transmission suggests different approaches to curing their ills other than focusing on managerial techniques or administrative solutions.

It may be that only well-differentiated leadership, supported by the hierarchy of stockholders, can reformat multigenerational influence. This is in stark contrast to the concept of "know-how." As with therapists, because of all the books and workshops now available on managerial and administrative techniques, everyone "knows how." Yet there are still only a very few really successful organizations in any field of endeavor. If the problem were know-how, we should see more successful institutions. Related here is the fact that Bowen's concept of transmission suggests a different classification principle for consulting with work systems. All institutions can be regrouped, and then compared, more significantly, according to longitudinal principles of differentiation and the multigenerational transmission of chronic anxiety, rather than separated into conventional sociological categories of function or product.

Finally, here is one small example of great illustrative consequence: In reviewing the family budget, a husband was showing his wife how he had several sources of income, and how he allocated funds from these various sources for different family expenses. The wife responded, "Why do you break it up that way? It's all one pot. There is no reason why this source should pay for that expense. You've made things unnecessarily complicated, and hidden the overall strength in that dichotomous approach." She suggested unifying procedures, and he resisted strongly, though he could give no logical reason why he insisted on maintaining the present pattern. Finally he said, "Things just evolved this way. As this source developed, I was able to justify this expense, and they just kind of 'grew up together.' " The principle that emerges from this illustration, and it is a principle that is equally applicable to all institutions, work, or family, is that *evolutionary flow has more power to format the structure of relationships than the* logic *of their contemporary connections.*

Emotional Triangles

A fourth essential Bowen concept is the idea of an emotional triangle. This refers to any three parts of an emotional system, either three individuals or two persons and an issue. Bowen has referred to triangles as the "molecules" of families, the basic building blocks. While the term is often shortened to "triangle," the concept is more complex than a triad. Emotional triangles have specific rules that govern their emotional processes, such as the idea that you cannot change a relationship between two others or between another person and his or her habit. They function perversely; the more you try to change the relationship of two others (again, either two other people or a person and his or her habit), the more likely it is that you will reinforce the very aspects of the relationship you want to change.

Kerr (1981) has suggested that triangles are natural phenomena, and certainly their universality would hint of that. They are not more prone to form in one culture than another, or in one century than another, nor are the rules they follow gender-specific in any way. He has also tried to show evidence of emotional triangles in other species. Bowen has suggested that triangles form out of the anxiety of two-person systems, that it is impossible for any two persons to maintain the level of differentiation necessary to retain a stable relationship, and that one way of stabilizing a relationship, therefore, is to draw a third party into it, either directly or by discussion. (How long can two people talk to each other without beginning to talk about a third?)

While the concept of an emotional triangle may not appear to have the theoretical weightiness of the three concepts discussed previously, it goes a long way towards supplying a method for linking and operationalizing the others. It has enormous clinical and administrative significance. For example, the concept of a triangle can help explain why systems do not change despite reorganization (e.g., centralization or decentralization) if that change fails to affect the relevant triangles. Similarly, the concept of an emotional triangle can go far towards explaining why change does not occur when new people enter an old system. What any newcomer to a family or a work system really enters is a set of previously established interlocking triangles, with all the emotional process that conveys. (The fact that triangles do not change when one of the parties leaves also explains why neither death, divorce, nor leaving home usually change family triangles.)

With regard to therapy, this central concept supplies a strategy in itself. It is that if you, as a therapist, allow a couple to create a triangle with you, but take care not to get caught up in the emotional process of that triangle either by overfunctioning or being emotionally reactive, then, *by trying to remain a nonanxious presence in that triangle, you can induce a change in the relationship of the other two that would not occur if they said the same things in your absence.* This procedure can function equally well in a work system, in therapy, or in one's own family.

Another major theoretical ramification of the concept of an emotional triangle is that it offers a different perspective on stress. One of the universal rules of triangles is that, to the extent that you become responsible for, or try to change the relationship of, two others — two people or a person and a habit — you will experience the stress for their relationship. The idea that *stress is positional rather than quantitative* has enormous consequence for the way people function in all their emotional systems. Just explaining this notion can often help highly stressed individuals to see changes they have to make far more easily than do efforts to have them understand personal qualities that are motivating them to remain in stressful dilemmas. It is, once again, a focus on the (vertical) response axis rather than on the (horizontal) condition axis. Because the concept of an emotional triangle emphasizes position rather than personality, it is a concept that belongs to field theory, and when one can see how various triangles interlock, sometimes one can almost see the entire field. Indeed, the opposite may also be true, that the failure to see the network of triangles, or how one is caught in a given triangle, results in more either/or thinking and blaming.

The concept of an emotional triangle, particularly of interlocking triangles, also helps plot the path of multigenerational transmission when viewing genograms and can help us see things as similar that we might otherwise treat as different. For example, far fewer mothers die in childbirth today, and that is certainly due in part to advances in medicine. But even at its worst point in recorded history, the majority of mothers did not die in childbirth. If the higher mortality rate years ago can be explained in terms of poor medicine alone, why were there not more deaths? On the other hand, the concept of an emotional triangle suggests the possibility that the same family position most conducive to postpartum depression today (which may have taken up the slack of many of those deaths) as well as to many modern birth-giving mortalities, namely, an emotional triangle between a passive or critical husband and a distant or critically dependent mother (of the new mother), was a major variable that influenced which mothers died and which mothers recovered from childbirth complications years ago. (There is implicit here an assumption that any patient's response to "complications" from any medical procedure, if not the manifestation of the complications themselves, is related to his or her differentiation.) Thus, the concept of an emotional triangle can identify similarities over the generations that one might otherwise not see if one focused on conventional sociological distinctions such as the age at which an event occurred.

The major clinical significance of the concept of an emotional triangle is that it focuses on phenomenology rather than interpretation. When Bowen left the psychoanalytic movement, one aspect of psychoanalysis that troubled him was its unverifiability. (See below regarding his concern for objectivity.) Interpretation of others' motivations is slippery stuff. The very process invites projection. In addition, motivation is irrelevant to determining the validity of an action, so there is the ever-present danger of *ad hominem* reasoning, that is, evaluating the worth of an action or an idea on the basis of an attribute, or the situation of the person making the statement, or the psychological reason why it was performed.

Clinically, the concept of an emotional triangle frees one from having to read minds. It keeps one focused on factors that are describable and veridical. And it enables one to gauge change in a manner that is less affected by the psyche of the observer. In short, the concept of an emotional triangle is tied up with the objectivity of the observer, and, as will be seen shortly, that is a major principle in the application of Bowen theory.

Bowen Therapy

As in the previous section on theory, the following discussion of Bowen therapy will focus primarily on what I perceive to be most characteristic and different — though what may be most characteristic and different is that Bowen theory tries not to emphasize any distinction between theory and therapy in the first place! This is precisely why supervision is aimed at the thinking and differentiation of the therapist rather than at teaching him or her a set of techniques. The assumption is that the therapist will be able to promote differentiation in a family (the ultimate aim of all Bowen therapy) to the extent that the therapist has promoted his or her own. Another way of saying this is, from the perspective of Bowen theory, that any technique has the potential to "work," and the same technique (reframing, restructuring, reconstruction, rituals, paradox, family of origin, use of gender issues, etc.) will have different results, depending less on its appropriateness for a given family situation, how it is employed, or the background, personality, gender, and style of the therapist, than on the degree of differentiation in the therapist employing it. As mentioned above, it is the "being" of the therapist, the therapist's presence rather than any specific behavior, that is the agent of change. That presence includes engaging without being reactive, stimulating without rescuing, and teaching a way of thinking and observing without willing the other's head to change. The power of the therapist is based more on the nature of the connectedness that comes with being human, that is, the nature of emotional systems, than on specific skills at fixing families. It is almost as though the verb "to be" were transitive, and one could, by the nature of one's being, *"be"* — that is, have an effect on — someone else.

Within the therapeutic encounter itself, there are not actually a lot of specific techniques to be taught. Coaching couples to be more self-defined, teaching people to be more objective about themselves in relation to their environment, tutoring about the principles of triangles, encouraging people to learn about their multigenerational emotional histories and to go back and face issues they have fled, reworking family cutoffs and teasing out, and challenging or encouraging the emergence of self are the basic pathways, and any that are promoted by a nonreactive therapist who is continuing to work on his or her own maturity are in the service of differentiation. Over the years, a body of specific ways to go about this has evolved and can be learned from any Bowen-trained therapist through example, supervision, or videotapes.

More important for this essay on differentiating differentiation than showing how to apply Bowen theory are some of the principles that underpin the application. As stated earlier, by the nature of the case, this entire essay has been weighted towards theory, not practice. *The theory was not prelude to the practice; thinking it is the practice!* The discussion of application that follows, therefore, is for the purpose of further clarifying the theory, rather than some culmination that describes how to do it. And the various clinical examples cited, therefore, should be understood as having this illustrative purpose rather than as instructions on the proper, no less the only, way to deal with that particular situation.

Three principles about the conduct of therapy that Bowen has tried to teach his disciples will be discussed. They have to do with (1) the objectivity of the therapist; (2) the effect of proximity on protoplasm, and; (3) a natural systems-based view of healing as a self-regenerative process. All fit logically within the framework of the major characteristics and theoretical constructs discussed above — though because of the emphasis on the being of the therapist, the concept of differentiation will be seen to occupy a position of increasingly central importance, unifying theory and therapy, therapeutic functioning and client functioning, and the three underlying principles themselves. As the major constructs, all three are interdependent so that none can be fully understood without some understanding of the other two. It will also be seen that Bowen therapy's construction of the therapeutic encounter forces a reframing of traditional questions about treatment strategies, therapeutic failure, and termination, and establishes different criteria for evaluating change.

Objectivity

Shortly after Bowen joined the Georgetown Medical School faculty, a story circulating in the wake of his pioneering studies with hospitalized families at the National Institutes of Mental Health (NIMH) was of a woman who had come to him for a pass to go home. According to the tale, she also asked for a prescription for sleeping pills, and as Bowen was writing out the prescription, she added that when she got home, she was going to use them to kill herself. As the story was told, Bowen just went on writing the prescription, and without even looking up, asked, "Well, just how many do you think you'll need?" In one version, she went home, took them out, immediately became nauseated, and flushed them down the toilet.

The story of that event, which occurred about thirty years ago, would be heard today as an early precursor of what has come to be called paradox, or what Bowen came to call a "reversal." His response was far more than an effort to affect the client, however. It was a manifestation of Bowen's own lifelong effort to maintain objectivity (a scientific attitude), which he has always seen as crucial to effective change. Indeed, he winds up taking the position that whatever promotes objectivity also promotes change and was led to this connection from the realization years after NIMH that "I did my best work with my research families."

Almost all schools of therapy have been concerned about objectivity, of course. What has been special about Bowen's approach to this universal quest is that he has seen the problem of objectivity as an emotional phenomenon and not as a cerebral or a sensory issue. Bowen's guideline is: *Objectivity is inversely proportional to reactivity.* As mentioned above regarding chronic anxiety, clearheadedness is an emotional state and is maximized when the therapist works on his or her own self-regulation, which is partly a function of differentiation and partly a function of staying detriangled. This way of thinking, which makes the achieving of objectivity dependent on the emotional being of the therapist rather than on his or her acuity of perception, or "powers of observation," is what unifies the factors that promote objectivity with those that promote healing.

To understand Bowen's response to the woman's provocative statement, one has to realize that within the perspective of Bowen theory the major thrust of paradoxical or any other "technique" in the application of the theory is less towards changing the head of the client than towards maintaining the differentiation (i.e., reducing the anxiety) of the therapist. Paradox is aimed at the paradoxer, to help keep him or her out of that pernicious triangle that subverts all well-intentioned therapeutic efforts: the triangle in which the therapist winds up stuck with the responsibility for the client's problem or destiny. It is here that objectivity and therapeusis become one. As was shown above, remaining in a triangle (here it is Bowen, the woman, and the responsibility for her life), but staying untriangled, is in itself a therapeutic stance. It follows, therefore, that *all detriangling procedures designed to maintain objectivity (differentiation) in the therapist automatically contribute to differentiation in the client.* In other words, the change process does not center on the behavioral functioning of the client, but on the same emotional functioning in the therapist that optimizes his or her objectivity. This also means that when a family appears to be stuck, the therapist should focus primarily on changing his or her own input into the therapeutic triangle. In addition, since most efforts on the part of a triangled therapist to will change in a client increase or stem from anxiety in either client or therapist, by remaining focused on issues in the therapeutic triangle, the therapist also promotes healing and objectivity simultaneously.

Bowen's reconceptualization of the problem of objectivity in terms of emotional triangles is also worth noting because it was, in some ways, his own effort to remain objective about the field of psychotherapy, as well as to stay out of one of its major (emotional) triangles. It is one more example of what is so often characteristic of his own thinking processes: his tendency to come in at a tangent to conventional dichotomies. In the 1950s, the range of therapeutic modalities was much narrower than it is today. Psychoanalysis and behaviorism were almost the only choices. They were not only different schools, but also different establishments. Psychoanalysis saw the objectivity problem in terms of transference: the tendency of the patient to reproduce in the relationship with the therapist the same system of responses, expectations, and fantasies that had been programmed (habituated) by his or her parents, and the countertransference, the phenomenon where the therapist either does likewise or falls into the trap of responding as the patient's parent had. Behaviorism tried to avoid the issues of "freedom and dignity" completely by treating the human animal as a laboratory animal (Skinner, 1971). Psychodynamics (and insight), the therapeutic relationship, and motivation were irrelevant; "contingencies of reinforcement," or conditioning, was *the* name of the game. Bowen avoided getting caught in that either/or by, on the one hand, honoring the concept of transference, while, on the other, trying to approach it from a laboratory — that is, a research — observer position.

Instead of considering the interpretation of the transference to be the key to change, which meant encouraging one to form, Bowen thought the therapist should try to *stay out* of the transference as much as possible by functioning in a detriangled manner that kept it fulminating within the family, in front of him. He was shifting the therapy setting, as he put it in an early presentation, "from couch to coach" (Bowen, 1978). And his guideline to the therapist who became too active, itself often a manifestation of anxiety, was, "Make yourself as small as possible in the session." As will be seen in the next section on proximity and protoplasm, "make yourself small" can have fundamentally significant consequences, not only for the objectivity of the therapist, but also for the very survival of a client.

With regard to the present matter of objectivity, "make yourself small" was a guideline to help the therapist adopt a "nonparticipant" vantage point outside the emotional field that would enable him or her to observe more objectively, that is, to distinguish process from content. In addition, the logic of the theory suggested that it would, at the same time, actually promote change faster than encouraging the transference, because the therapist would be less likely to absorb, or to be absorbed into, the family emotional system. The therapist was, of course, partic-ipating, but as a catalyst. And catalyst means, by definition, something that by its presence fosters a reaction between other elements that cannot occur in its absence but which maintains its own integrity by not be-coming lost in the process. This is also, of course, the perfect detriangled involvement.

To appreciate how radically different the idea of staying out of the transference was in its day, one might compare it to the position of Reinman and other nineteenth-century geometricians who broke with Euclid's fundamental ideas on parallel lines, saying, "If space is curved, there are no such things as parallel lines." In other words, a basic pos-tulate was not discarded as much as it was turned on its head. And, just as in geometry, where that simple-appearing, non-Euclidian change in a basic premise led to viewing things in a new dimension (and, down the line, to relativity and a guide for interplanetary travel), so the concept of staying out of the transference led Bowen to seeing the client in a new dimension and to an entirely new adventure in comprehending the human condition: systemic family therapy. (Bowen has described part of his own intellectual odyssey in his epilogue to Kerr's [1988] *Family Evaluation.*)

As in so much of Bowen theory, precisely because it is a basic shift in conceptualizing, the idea of "staying out of the transference" cannot be easily classified by the standard conventions of psychotherapy. The position is akin neither to that of insight nor to that of behaviorism. It preserves the power inherent in the therapeutic presence, but emphasizes the factors that will make that presence objective. What also makes the concept of staying out of the transference difficult to comprehend is that it can sound like a prescription for doing nothing. But, as already mentioned, the truth is quite the contrary. The art is to remain a part of the triangle without getting "triangled," that is, without becoming either a focus of the others' displacement, a conduit for their connection, or reactive to their relationship. That requires a kind of balance and self-regulation similar to walking a tightrope — while someone is standing there shaking it. It must be added, however, that a detriangling maneuver after one has been caught for a while, wittingly or unwittingly, in a family system seems to have freeing effects similar to what follows in the resolution of a transference.

There are a variety of methods that Bowen-trained therapists have learned to use to foster an objective state: mischievous, paradoxical responses; avoiding interpretations; diagramming the family on a blackboard; telling (disguised) stories about other clients as protective techniques; and making clear one's own positions. But the major "technique" that Bowen and his disciples have taught as *the way to maintain such an objectivity and differentiation-promoting position is simply to ask questions.* One might even say that the major "intervention" in Bowen family therapy is a question. Questions are a marvelous way of staying in touch with someone without becoming responsible for the person or the person's dilemmas. Also, as long as you are the one asking the questions, you cannot be the overfunctioning expert giving all the answers. After a while, you learn that questions are quite subversive of mindsets and often have more staying power than suggestions for new behavior. For example, one might ask a single woman who says she does not date because her family taught her that men were weak and she does not want to hurt them: "Would you be willing to take a month and see how many men you could destroy?" Or, to an overfunctioning, perpetually deadline-giving father who has just given his son six weeks to shape up: "Why not five?" Then you come to realize that sometimes you can ask the "wrong" person a question (a three-cornered shot, so to speak), so that the one you really want to hear (be objective about) the informational content of the sentence will overhear it (louder) because his or her defenses have been outflanked. For example, to a married woman in front of her frustrating, passive-aggressive husband, the question might be: "What gets stirred up in you when your husband acts like such a wimp?" Or to a father in front of his arguing wife and son: "Can your son seduce his mother into an argument anytime he wants?"

Questions, obviously, can also be a form of challenge, as in the question to any family member who is acting helpless in the face of a relative's initiatives: "What would it take for you to become less vulnerable to his/her remarks (actions)?" And challenge is a way of promoting growth without increasing dependency and subjectivity. In other words, questions are inherently detriangling maneuvers. Sometimes the question in "reversal" form can sharpen awareness by paradoxing the whole therapeutic encounter, as when clients report in a self-satisfied manner that they are doing better and the Bowen-oriented therapist responds in a calm, inquisitive manner, "Could you make it go back to the way it was? How would you go about it?" Pursuing the subject diligently, the therapist thus gets the clients to think out the problem carefully and respond searchingly, and with thoughtful deliberation, to one another's suggestions for regression, and why they think "that" would no longer work. Talk about staying out of the transference! Who ever had a parent nonanxious enough to invite planning for making things worse?

Other schools have emphasized the use of questions, of course, but rarely because of their effect on the emotional field between therapist and client or because of the objectivity-promoting stance and self-regulation they promote in the poser! This is not to say that the information obtained by asking these questions is unimportant — quite the contrary. As Bowen has emphasized, "the more I learn about the family, the more they learn." This attitude fits the basic research orientation he has tried to recapture since the pioneering days at NIMH. But how information, the "message," is perceived by the therapist, or the family, depends on the emotional system, the *medium* in which it is transmitted. And that depends on the degree of differentiation (or the opposite, the degree of anxiety) in the field, which, in turn, depends primarily on the emotional being of the therapist. From the perspective of Bowen theory, therefore, *when it comes to promoting change, clarity may be more important than empathy,* not only because helping people to be objective about their position in life automatically contributes to their healing, but also because it is only when a therapist's orientation is concerned with clarity that he or she may distinguish empathy from anxiety.

Proximity and Protoplasm

Around 1970, Bowen was seeing a family once a month and recording the interviews for training. The wife was given to serious breakdowns in her functioning and had been hospitalized several times. During one of these interviews, the husband, a very concerned and sensitive (if also somewhat passive) man, was describing how no amount of effort on his part to understand his wife seemed to make any difference. At this point, Bowen responded that he did not think it would ever again be possible for husbands and wives to understand one another. The next tape showed the couple six months later. The woman was no longer depressed and was going about her daily business bright and cheerful as if she had been relieved from shouldering some tremendous burden. As Bowen asked the couple questions designed to find out how the change had come about, the husband volunteered, "I've stopped trying to understand her."

At about that same time, a research project was taking place that was concerned with very similar emotional phenomena and that ultimately may prove to have more significance for the application of Bowen theory than will his own work at NIMH. It was not research with human families, however, but with a much smaller form of protoplasm. In 1970, the results were published of an extremely sophisticated experiment in which organisms from a species that had not evolved immune systems *(gorganzoa)* were moved towards one another in increasingly greater degrees of proximity (Theodore, 1970). It was known that creatures of the same species that do not have immune systems will fuse upon contact and become one organism since the immune system is basically the capacity to distinguish self from nonself. Indeed, without immunologic systems, there would be no existential category of self (Thomas, 1974). We need them not only to ward off enemies, but also in order to love, that is, touch. The other side of transplant rejection is the capacity for self-differentiation. In this experiment, what was observed was that at a certain distance, the smaller organism began to disintegrate, and within twenty-four hours had lost the principles of its organization completely. Careful controls proved that the larger one had done nothing to do the other in, either through the secretion of substances or through any form of frontal attack. The disintegration of the smaller organism was purely the result of its own metabolic mechanisms functioning reactively to the *proximity* of the other. *The experimenters had "induced auto-destruction" by moving the creatures closer to a member of their own species.* While one might be tempted to blame the larger for not giving its partner enough distance, that misses the most important dimension of this (emotional) phenomenon. Had the disintegrating partner been able to develop more capacity to discriminate self from nonself (worked on its own vulnerability to the other), it might have been able to tolerate more proximity.

The ramifications of this finding for human protoplasm are extraordinary. They suggest that the major problem of families may not be to get members to be closer, but to enable them to be clearer about where they end and others in their life begin. Most of the helping professions seem to be largely concerned with promoting proximity rather than differentiation, despite the fact that the natural movement of protoplasm seems to be towards other protoplasm. In other words, *the basic problem in families may not be to maintain relationships but to maintain the self that permits nondisintegrative relationships.*

Two different comments from women clients reflect the opposite ends of this emotional phenomenon. One, thinking back on how she had lost the self that was now reemerging, said, "The day I got married, I disappeared." The other, upon finally seeing some evidence that her partner's self was emerging, said, "When my husband said, 'I,' suddenly there were two of us." This is more than an issue of "boundaries," as some like to put it. It is *existential* in the deepest sense of the term. It gets to the very essence of protoplasm and the essential nature of anxiety. Of course, with human organisms we are dealing with a far more complex understanding of space and size. The issue of the smaller or larger organism gets played out in families not in terms of avoirdupois, but rather in categories of over- and underfunctioning. *Nothing fuses people like one overfunctioning in the other's space, whereas nothing creates emotional space like self-definition.* It is here, by the way, that we can distinguish more clearly the concept of *fusion* as used by Bowen and *enmeshment* as used by the structural school. *All fusion involves enmeshment, but there is in the biological concept of fusion the additional sense of the loss of the organism's integrity,* the principles that give it coherence. Thus, fusion can have a positive valence or a negative one (homey togetherness or perpetually reactive argumentativeness). Similarly, we gain another way of comprehending differentiation. Autonomy or individuation can be conceived of as an external spatial phenomenon, in which case it can be accomplished without concern for the inner coherence provided by integrity; differentiation cannot.

An enormous number of "individual" symptoms, both physical and "psychological," take on new meaning when viewed in the context of the loss of self in a relationship. The notion that proximity can induce autodestruction in one partner to a relationship when there is no capacity for an immunologic response (either because of the degree of fusion between them or because there was not enough self to permit it) opens the door to viewing all chronic conditions that manifest themselves in one relative as byproducts of the fusion that characterizes their relationship with each other. This perspective on "individual" symptoms ultimately sets the groundwork for (1) making the promotion of differentiation (that is, the capacity for an immunologic response) the basic healing strategy for any symptomatic person no matter what the nature of the symptom (with cancer patients, it almost may be conceptualized as a holistic approach to imagery); and (2) working with the nonsymptomatic spouse (or parent or child) when the symptomatic family member is the underfunctioner. For, as Bowen has taught, it is very difficult to get the underfunctioner to move until the overfunctioner (who luckily also tends to be the more motivated one) can reduce his or her overfunctioning, that is, can "make himself or herself smaller."

These notions about proximity, protoplasm, and anxiety also have fundamentally significant ramifications for the therapeutic relationship. They suggest that responses from helping professionals such as rescuing and supporting not only may be counterproductive, "enabling," or codependent, but may, if the helper overfunctions enough, actually induce autodestruction, that is, dis-"integr"-ation in the client. It is in this context that we can fully appreciate the fundamental significance of Bowen's admonition to the therapist to "make yourself small." And it is here that we can see how essentially connected are the differentiating processes that promote objectivity and those that promote well-being.

Overall, the proximity/protoplasm perspective suggests that *fusion with a client has more toxic potential than lack of empathy,* and that *anxiety in the helper can be more damaging than even sexual contact* (which sin we would all prefer to focus on). All this brings us back to the idea that the health of the client begins with, and cannot go beyond, the level of differentiation achieved by the helper.

Translated into practice, the proximity/protoplasm factor means that the therapist, instead of trying to will togetherness directly, might promote it more effectively by encouraging the self (differentiation) of the individual members, because, as Bowen once put it, "A self is more attractive than a no-self." (Another Bowenism that captures the same paradox of togetherness is that in any relationship the one doing the *least* amount of thinking about the other tends to be the one who is more attractive to the other.) In other words, people do not have to be taught how to get closer. Moving towards others is natural. Anything, therefore, that a therapist can do on the side of differentiation — challenging self, reducing anxiety, encouraging reconnection with one's own family of origin, and the like — is not opposed to togetherness, even if it is initially perceived in that way by others who have temporarily lost a part of their selves in their relative's progress, but is really in its cause. The issue is far deeper than effectiveness, of course. It relates, rather, to how togetherness can be promoted in a manner that minimizes the sacrifice of integrity of all family members and the consequent recycling of symptomatology within the family that accompanies such loss. The issue of integrity is not merely a matter of compromise or ethics, but probably a condition that minimizes carcinogenesis, or any other dis-"integr"-ative process. The bottom line is that whenever you increase togetherness without also increasing self-differentiation, you run the risk of losing that togetherness through the autodestruction of one of the partners.

Here is an example of one way I have found to convey the connection between proximity and self in a clinical situation familiar to any family therapist, the one in which an overfunctioning woman is on the verge of burnout, or worse, because she has allowed herself to become triangled into taking responsibility for every relationship in her family. She is usually thinking of separation, perhaps even of abandoning her children. Both options run contrary to her values of family togetherness, yet she also can no longer carry the burden and the frustration of the togetherness they have. She may be perceived as controlling in her effort to preserve the family, but her perceived controllingness is really an adaptation in which she has sacrificed enormous amounts of her own self to the mindless control of her family's emotional processes. (It is amazing how little control people have over the way they control others.)

I begin by drawing a large circle representing her with the other members of her family as smaller intersecting squares and circles. "This is the family," I say. Then I erase those parts of the smaller circles and squares that have crossed over her line, and add, "This is the outline of yourself." (One woman with uncommon perceptiveness said, "They look like lesions.")

Next, I ask, "Would you be willing to try to move your circle outside the intersections and complete the outline of yourself over there, away from them, but keep relating to them from outside their space?" She is warned, however, that all of the other creatures in her life will immediately feel her pullout from the fusion as taking some of their cells along with her. Predictably, they will react characteristically to their gaping wound, responding automatically to glob her back into the togetherness according to the way they have been wont to do in the past. They will, in short, have symptoms for togetherness. Most people can tell you exactly what that symptom in their partner, child, or parent will be (drinking, spending, getting sick, having an affair, having an accident, becoming hypercritical, running away from home, etc.). But, this woman is told, if she can contain her anxiety and learn how to be nonreactive to the sabotage (the reactivity of others), which means staying on course for her own differentiation without cutting off (often by maintaining a mischievous-response mode), there is a more than likely chance that the others will succeed in closing their own wounds, and then everyone can relate to one another as better-defined individuals from outside one another's space. (The nonreactive stance is often best maintained through a mischievous-response mode: "Honey, there's a sale on your favorite Scotch across town." "Why are you telling me that?" "Well, remember that job that you said if I took it, you'd leave? I took it.")

This is really a form of leadership (the same diagrams can be drawn for the burdened, frustrated leader of any organization), and it can be a very powerful form of medicine, but not for those who prefer peace to progress. Actually, once a Bowen-coached client begins to move into a differentiating mode, more time is probably spent, at first, in learning how to deal with the sabotage than in learning how to differentiate. Interestingly, *the major variable in the outcome (cutoff, reglobbing, or a more differentiated togetherness) seems to be the adroitness and persistence of the differentiating partner, not the degree of reactivity or severity of the symptom in the family member wanting to de-differentiate the relationship.* What can be said with some surety is this: the togetherness that results from an approach that emphasizes self-differentiation rather than "cooperation" usually tends to be more lasting, to be less vulnerable to future changes or regressions in either partner, and to be characterized by healthier (noncritical) interchanges. This is probably true because the togetherness that results is not based on increasing the emotional dependencies and is not an adaptation to the symptom, but evolves out of the increasing self-reliance and strengths of the partners. And the same can be true for parents differentiating from their children, or from their own parents.

Finally, as this coaching example illustrates, the understanding of proximity and protoplasm being presented here is consistent with the previously mentioned emphasis throughout Bowen theory on focusing on the strength in a family. This idea will now be further reinforced by the notion that healing is a natural (that is, a self-regenerative) process.

Healing as a Self-Regenerative Phenomenon

The most crucial concept in understanding and practicing Bowen therapy is his view that healing is a self-regenerative process. Self-regenerative means not only self-responsible, but also self-actualizing. The act of taking responsibility for one's own emotional being and destiny is not only the key to survival, but that very attitude creates the self that is the necessary resource for that end.

I began to appreciate the centrality of this notion to all of Bowen's thinking from the very beginning of my association with him (1967) as a result of two events that occurred in consecutive supervision sessions. The context of one was the relationship between therapist and patient and the context of the other was the relationship between supervisor and therapist, but the concepts were essentially the same.

In the first situation, a colleague suddenly interrupted our session with a call from a mental hospital. She had gotten herself institution-alized by sending the anxiety of her internist through the roof with her outlandish fantasies. She was now complaining that they were trying to get her with gas fumes sent through the ventilators. Avoiding the content of her fears, whether or not they were true or she was crazy, Bowen responded, "Gertrude, you can think as crazy as you want, but if you don't stop talking about it, they're going to commit you." She was out the next day.

At the time, I simply focused on his foxiness. In one masterful stroke, Bowen had stayed out of the triangle with her craziness, declined the gambit of her perversity, reframed the entire issue into a category that she could do something about, and made her responsible for her own condition, if not her destiny.

The following week, I saw that something much deeper was involved than Bowen's adroitness. This time the issue was my own concerns. I was worried about the fact that I could not be covered by malpractice insurance until I was eligible to join one of the recognized therapy asso-ciations. This time his response was, "Malpractice is most likely to occur when the professional gives too much promise." As I considered the nov-elty of thinking about malpractice litigation as a breach-of-promise suit, I suddenly realized that he was asking me to deal with my anxieties in the same manner as he had dealt with his patient, to focus on my own input and, in the process, to behave towards the problem in a manner that was self-regulatory. Eventually, I came to realize that this focus on responsibility for self, and *his confidence that in promoting its actualiza-tion he was optimizing the conditions for healing processes to do their work,* was the logical bottom line of a natural systems orientation to both healing and pathology. "Natural" means that both are driven by the same universal forces that describe life everywhere, and "systems" means they are part of one another. This self-regenerative perspective changes the entire thrust of therapy; crisis or illness, instead of being "merely" an anxious occasion to be fixed, now becomes an opportunity for the growth of the client as well as the evolution of the species. And it changes the criterion for deciding which member of a family to work with from who has the symptom to who is most motivated to continue the pursuit of differentiation. The logic of the paradigm is as follows.

A True Paradigm Shift

A Natural Systems View of Pathology

The characteristic that all pathogens have in common is the absence of a factor that regulates their own growth and behavior. While this is most obviously true in malignancy, where, unlike "normal" cells, malignant cells fail to differentiate, specialize, or limit their proliferation, it is the same with families, organizations, and civilization itself. Whether one is considering an acting-out child, an obstreperous, given-to-tantrums, or tyrannical family member; whether one is considering members of an organization who persistently try to bend everyone to their will; or whether one is observing a totalitarian nation, what is always true about such forces is that they never will say no to themselves. They, of course, have no self apart from their behavior to say no to. It is precisely this inability to differentiate that gives to viruses, abusers, and totalitarian states their infectious, invasive, or malignant quality.

This same inability to regulate self not only contributes to unregulated growth, but it also prevents the growth we call maturity. Bowen has, in fact, often substituted the word "immaturity" for "pathology." After all, creatures without the capacity to regulate their own behavior cannot learn from their experience. This is why reasoning with (immature) human troublemakers is as effective as reasoning with a virus. It is also this lack of a self-regulatory factor that makes it natural for pathogens to pass their own functioning on, unmodified, from generation to generation. An interesting natural systems parallel exists between multigenerational transmission of pathology (that is, immaturity) in cancerous processes and in families with acting-out children. In vitro studies of leukemic cells have shown that where the missing growth (regulatory) protein can be reinserted into the malignant cells, the transmission of their malignant characteristic to the next generation immediately ceases (Sachs, 1986). Bowen-trained therapists tend not to see children but to work with the parents *instead*. This is a very similar form of intervention, as there is no such thing as acting-out children with mature parents, and when the parents can learn to be better differentiated (and in that process to be more self-regulative), the transmission of immaturity to the next generation often ceases. More than that, interfering with the transmission from one generation to the next in this way stops metastasis into society.

Pathogens, however, never do it alone. There is always another self-regulation issue involved in the creation of pathology, the failure on the part of the host. This brings us to a second natural characteristic of all pathological processes. Pathology is less the result of the presence of the pathogen than the product of its replication. To a very large extent, pathological processes (physical or relational) that continue are simply those that are tolerated by the surrounding "cells." Oncogenesis does not have to result in the disease we call cancer. Indeed, the development of all life may have as much to do with relationships as with essence, since recent studies have shown that cells develop, particularly in the embryonic stage, not only according to their own DNA, but also according to what adjacent cells will permit them to do.

Bowen therapy is about the immunologic response. It is a focus on strength rather than weakness, on the evolution of self that is necessary for its expression and on the self-regulation that keeps the opposite extreme, autoimmunity (reactivity), in check.

The concept is just as applicable to work systems. I have found that the leader of any organization functions as its immunologic system; to the extent that he or she is well-defined (meaning, primarily, clear and nonreactive), the pathogens, though present, are far less likely to replicate. And, once again, there is a natural systems parallel. Recently, it was discovered that our nerves communicate not only electrically to that which is contiguous, but also chemically to other, relatively distant parts of the body through the release of substances called neurotransmitters that dock at appropriate receptor sites. With this discovery has come the awareness that the brain is the largest organ of secretion in the body, and that its main function might be to preserve the health of the organism (thinking may be a bonus). For every neurotransmitter thus far discovered that is released by the brain, the appropriate receptor site exists in the immunologic system, and vice versa (Pert, 1986). And this ties back to the previously mentioned concept of leadership through self-differentiation, that the functioning of the "head" has a systemic effect on the body (politic) that can be far more influential than what the "head" actually says to its followers.

A Natural Systems View of Healing

Implicating the good guys in the course of pathological processes brings us around to the other side of self-regulation. If the essence of pathology is its absence, the process that leads to health is its development, *not in the pathogenic force, however, but in the organism's response.* (This is a focus on the vertical axis rather than the horizontal one in the bipolar graph.) Bowen's views of the way to promote such self-regulation have also been influenced by two natural systems processes. One is that life moves towards life. In other words, life does not have to be taught how to do it. The second is that the processes of maturation have their own time frame. Not only can they often not be speeded up, but sometimes it is necessary, as with fermentation or embryonic development, to slow processes down in order to gain the best results. Both of these views have significant technical ramifications for the conduct of therapy and are joined around the issue of anxiety, since it requires lowering one's anxiety to allow these processes to go their natural way, yet faith in their capacity to know their job can also lower one's anxiety about having to do something about it oneself.

Bowen's confidence in the natural order of things is similar to Einstein's. He almost seems to be making a statement about life's forces similar to that which Einstein made about physical forces, "I don't believe God plays dice with the Universe." The healer, in other words, does not have to take responsibility for making health happen, but for discovering the universal forces that make life tick, and then lining up the client's thinking and functioning with those life-sustaining forces that have continuously evolved since Creation. One may, therefore, have "faith" in natural processes. You can trust them, and having the confidence to rely on them can free any healer to defocus the symptom and the attending anxiety and refocus his or her own efforts on becoming a healing presence, that is, one who tries to promote healing rather than to will it.

This commitment to natural processes, by the way, was probably one of the factors that kept Bowen from joining those in the early days of the family movement who kept inveighing against the "medical model" because of its diagnosis of individuals. From Bowen's perspective, it was more likely psychiatry that had broken with the medical model, which, as he understood it, was a model that sought to describe life with the facts of nature rather than the subjectivity of metaphor.

From a natural systems perspective, the healing presence functions primarily in two ways: it inhibits the inhibitors and it stimulates the resources. The physician, for example, does not sew your cells together; he or she works primarily in two directions, to inhibit that which prevents them from doing what comes naturally (reducing inflammation, for example) or to initiate processes that need a jump start, for example, by injecting a weak form of the very virus that is the enemy in order to flag the T cells. Carried over to therapeutic functioning, what that means is (1) reducing the chronic anxiety that inhibits healing in emotional illness in exactly the same manner that inflammation inhibits physical healing, primarily by *being* a well-differentiated, nonanxious presence; and (2) stimulating the organism's own resources, which means guiding or challenging the self of the client to emerge. (Bowen has taught that what makes any paradoxical or challenging remark a weak or strong form of the live virus is the investment and anxiety in the healer.)

This focus on aiding the release of natural processes and on healers applying their will primarily to their own self-regulation, rather than to the regulation of others, has important ramifications for the major therapeutic problem of resistance. A natural systems orientation to healing helps minimize that inflammatory, sabotaging reactivity.

It does not take much experience in the field to see that the most intense forms of family symptomatology (anorexia, suicide, schizophrenia, abuse, violence, and many chronic physical diseases, not to mention a whole catalogue of marital and parent-child issues) tend to occur in families characterized by extreme will conflict, by which I mean that members of the family are constantly trying to will one another to adapt to their will rather than applying their will to their own self-differentiation. Willing others to change is, by definition, loss of self in the relationship. What often happens is that family will struggles become extended, like some huge hydrocarbon chain, into the therapeutic encounter where therapists get into willing their clients to stop willing other family members. And supervisors try willing their supervisees to stop willing their clients. All willing of others immediately creates an emotional triangle, of course, since it puts the willer between the willed one and that person's own will or habit. That is enough reason to understand its ineffectiveness. But willing others is also generally a reactive phenomenon. Willing clients to change, therefore, is not only usually ineffective, but it tends to excite the very inflammatory processes that prevent natural healing processes from doing their work.

Conversely, issues of resistance in therapy tend to fall away when therapists focus their will on their own self-differentiation, and when their focus on natural systems processes disengages them from that struggle. One of Bowen's guidelines for staying out of will conflict, which is related to overfunctioning responsibility and anxiety, has been that he takes responsibility for what happens in his office but not for what happens between sessions. My own way of putting it to therapists has been, "All healing that depends on the functioning of the healer rather than of the client is faith healing."

The second natural process basic to what Bowen has taught about therapy is that the process of maturation takes time. It cannot be willed or even speeded up beyond its own time frame. This notion also ties back in a similar way to the basic issue of anxiety, both the client's and the healer's.

The relationship between time and healing has two important consequences for therapeutic functioning. One has to do with the frequency and length of the therapeutic encounter, and the other with criteria for evaluating change. Since Bowen theory does not equate change with symptom relief or feeling better, but with an increase in the differentiation level of the family, it has a long-range perspective. Bowen-trained therapists, therefore, tend to be less concerned about the frequency of sessions than about the length of time a family stays in the process. Thus, families are rarely seen more frequently than biweekly, and as they increase the management of their own anxiety and self-directedness, often every third or fourth week, or, eventually, even several times a year. Longevity in the therapeutic contact promotes deeper involvement with multigenerational processes, and the emotional change discussed above that seems to be a prerequisite to any new patterns of thinking or behavior having the capacity to maintain a differentiating effect is just not something that fits into a timetable. That kind of emotional shift requires that some member of the family be committed to the process of differentiation for several years. From a conventional perspective, this approach may appear to encourage dependency, but Bowen theory again comes in at a tangent. Dependency may be more connected to frequency than to longevity, because if there is too little time between sessions, the therapist's presence cannot be differentiated from the change process. Dependency on the therapist, therefore, may be less a function of how long one goes to the "doctor" than of whether or not such visits are continuing to promote further differentiation, for example, by helping the client stay in touch with a particular way of thinking. Theoretically, this also means that "terminating therapy," as the phrase is usually used, makes little sense in this context. Dependency that continues to promote differentiation is, after all, by nature not dependency as that term normally connotes. A coach can be helpful even with decreasingly frequent contact as long as one plays the game.

However, the key to the dependency issue may really have very little to do with time intervals and much more to do with a shift in the differentiation of the client. When clients start wondering whether or not to continue, I draw an arrow on the board that has a zero in the middle.

"This is the arrow of progress," I say. "When clients first come in, they are way over to the right, meaning that they are highly anxious, constantly reactive with little self-regulation of their direction in life. When they wonder whether to continue, they have finally reached zero. Zero is characterized by the loss of the pain that originally motivated them to come in, but also the loss of that same stimulus for continuing to work on themselves." If they wish to continue to try to move their progress past zero, and I always suggest cutting the frequency of the sessions at that point, then two gains are probable. One is less likelihood of regression, and the second is, if regression does occur, that one can usually get it back to the furthest point one had previously reached.

Actually, much larger questions are raised by this emphasis on longevity rather than frequency. The notion of weekly visits to a therapist is, of course, simply convention, as is the notion that therapy should be outside the context of learning. For the past several years, I have been conducting a seminar in family emotional process for ordained clergy that has forced my faculty and me to question both assumptions. The "training" program meets three times a year for three consecutive days.

(It is based on a similar program Bowen conducts on a four-times-a-year basis for therapists.) One day is devoted to the parishioner family, one day to the congregation as a family, and one day to the members of clergy's own families of origin. The mornings are theoretical and the afternoons clinical. Only half of one day is actually devoted to what might conventionally be called "therapy," the afternoon of the third day, when we subdivide into family of origin groups. Yet the changes in emotional functioning that we have been seeing in the people attending are certainly equal to those we have observed in clients who are seen biweekly for a year or more. The only way we have been able to explain the depth of the changes we are observing (aside from the fact that by selection we are dealing with a very motivated group) is that the three perspectives when projected simultaneously seem to have a holographic effect, with the result that those in the training programs find every aspect of their emotional lives perceivable in greater depth throughout the year (not just during the nine days) because of the added dimensions. But it is Bowen theory that makes this possible by putting all three systems on the same "wavelength."

The second practical therapeutic ramification of allowing natural processes to develop in their own time is the time frame that should be used for evaluating change. Bowen has taught that it takes four years to change a family, that is, to modify its emotional processes to the point that the multigenerational transmission will not automatically continue into the next generation — and four years is not a guarantee. The multigenerational transmission perspective also probably means that evaluation of change requires a perspective of several generations. Since one obviously cannot wait that long, Bowen theory's emphasis on differentiation suggests two criteria for making predictions about how fundamental any change in a family may be that is outside the criterion of time. First, to the extent that any change in a nuclear family goes along with a change one of the partners made with his or her own family of origin, it is *more* likely to be a fundamental change. Second, any change that occurs because family members have become more adaptive to the symptom or the symptom-bearer is *less* likely to last than if the symptom goes away because the family has become less fused into it.

All of this brings us full circle to the differentiation of the therapist, because for the therapist to be willing to go along for that long requires a commitment to the same fundamental processes that are a premise of Bowen theory to begin with: self-differentiation and the evolution of our species. In other words, unless therapists are committed to the ongoing process of their own growth, they are not likely to have the emotional stamina to endure. The power of self-differentiation for promoting natural healing processes cannot be underestimated. The track record of many healers, marriage counselors, or oncologists shows too much willingness to quit when the going gets rough. Sometimes, it appears to be a lack of persistence, sometimes a failure to realize that one has the most power in a relationship precisely when one is ready to quit, and sometimes it just seems to be a morbid fatalism (disguising anxiety). For years I wondered what it was that differentiated the more motivated. Then one day I realized that it was something more essential to self, something Bowen had always taught more by the example of his life than through any specific lesson. I had been discussing with a client who had worked through some very difficult problems what distinguished those who succeed in changing their life course. Since he was a former boxer, I used an analogy from his sport and said that I thought it was the capacity to "take a punch." To my surprise and enlightenment, he responded, "You've got it wrong. It's not the *capacity* to take a punch; it's loving it." This is also what Bowen has taught: loving the struggle, being challenged by life to hang in there and find new ways to think about and approach its problems.

To recapitulate: Family therapy from Bowen's perspective emphasizes a way of thinking rather than a set of techniques. This emphasis is equally appropriate for the training of therapists, the conduct of therapy, or the coaching of clients regarding their functioning in their own emotional systems (family or work). Supervision, therapy, leadership, and growth thus become one. The approach is rooted in a natural systems concept of disease and healing that gives the theory an internal consistency. Thus, if personality, psychodynamics, and cultural background are not important in understanding family emotional process, neither are they the determining factors in the functioning of the therapist. The transcendent notion always is self-differentiation, which is understood to be the decisive variable in the etiology and cure of all emotional problems and the conduct of successful therapy (or supervision), and, in the end, the key to the evolution of our species (from a natural systems perspective, the ultimate purpose of all family therapy). In addition, the focus on the differentiation of the therapist as the key to therapeutic technique unifies objectivity and healing. When all is said and done, however, how you want your client to function in his or her relationships with others must characterize your own functioning in your relationship with your client — not because the client will learn to copy you, but because the emotional field in which you both operate must be conducive to further differentiation.

Bowen and Societal Regression

There is one more part to Bowen theory — its application to society and society's way of understanding itself. Indeed, the most significant aspect of Bowen theory may not lie in its therapeutic potential for a given family, but rather in its power to reformat the knowledge conventions of the social sciences and so influence what therapists see. And this may be still one more example of Bowen theory's uniqueness, the lens it supplies for looking at its own field.

In these concluding remarks, I shall describe briefly Bowen's concept of *societal regression,* its relevance for the field of family therapy (actually for all the helping professions), and the shift in social science thinking Bowen theory says is necessary before change artists can have an effect on society's own emotional processes. As will be seen, his views on this matter have influenced his functioning in the field.

If Bowen used universal concepts of life to understand families, he also reversed that perspective and asked what we can learn about society at large from what our concentrated focus on the family has reciprocally elucidated about life. It is not that society can be reduced to its molecular components (families), but rather that the same emotional forces are at work in both fields. Applying his major concepts to civilization, Bowen developed a concept he called "societal regression." Through this concept he has viewed society as a family, that is, as an emotional system, complete with its own multigenerational transmission, chronic anxiety, emotional triangles, cutoffs, projection processes, and fusion/differentiation struggles.

Bowen's concept of societal regression states that all of civilization goes through peaks and valleys in the curve of its own anxiety. Once again, the anxiety that is important is the chronic anxiety transmitted through the generations rather than its specific foci in a given age. As Kerr has put it, it is what exists *between* people rather than *in* them. In this view, phenomena such as increasing divorce rates, cults, the drug culture, inflation, and rampant diseases (plagues, tuberculosis, influenza, cancer, AIDS), and perhaps also the increase in homosexuality, can be viewed as symptoms of more anxious periods. In addition, as with any emotional system, "the family of man" also has its pet foci around which its free-floating anxiety will tend to crystalize: communists in one age, carcinogens in another; recombinant DNA in one generation, nuclear war in another; and so on through cholesterol, conservation issues, and ozone holes. Bowen's view regarding these crises in the human family was the same as with any family: try to minimize reactivity and maximize objectivity. Take care not to get caught up in the world's emotional system; these problems, too, will go their way if handled objectively — sometimes because we find solutions, but often because they simply seem to spend themselves or disappear from view when we get focused elsewhere. Above all, stay grounded in your own continued self-differentiation. This is precisely what Bowen has tried to practice with regard to the family of family therapists.

While annual conferences of some major family therapy associations have grown from five hundred to five thousand, Georgetown family therapy symposia went from fifteen hundred in the late 1970s to one-tenth that number in the 1990s. But it is not simply the variety or the competition that has decreased Georgetown attendance. *Bowen wanted it that way.* He feared that much of family therapy's popularity is a fad, itself symptomatic of societal anxiety. Since it is the nature of symptoms to recycle, Bowen did not want his theory to vanish in the next transformation. As a result, Bowen practiced the same effort at self-differentiation with regard to the family of family therapists that he recommended to any therapist or family member. He tried to maintain a separateness from the rest of the field that would enable him to continue the development of his own thinking. He, therefore, became more concerned with the development of his theory than with its relevance to any specific, contemporary problem.

From the perspective of Bowen theory, family therapy has failed to differentiate itself sufficiently from the very anxiety that produces the problems it seeks to cure. Societal regression, therefore, far from being ameliorated by the field of family therapy, is reflected in its own emotional system. According to this view, the anxiety shows up (1) in the way family therapy has aped consultation methods everywhere, focusing on administrative and managerial techniques and pursuing data indiscriminately rather than focusing on emotional processes and the self-regulation and growth of the therapist; and (2) more importantly, as I shall elaborate below, in family therapy's unquestioning acceptance of the paradigm of either/or dichotomies that characterizes all social science conceptualization.

An example of the former, again from the perspective of Bowen theory, is the manner in which new issues (or symptoms) constantly come into view, occupy center stage for a while, and then exit to the wings of some archive. In the 1970s, almost no family therapy conference was without a speaker on sexual dysfunction. Then, in rather rapid succession, the foci switched to cults, divorce, anorexia, gender issues, violence, substance abuse, and so on. Another example is the way in which therapeutic orientations also rapidly shift; for a while, it was epistemology, then in succession, paradox, circularity, family of origin, ethnicity, feminism, rituals, object relations, and constructionism. Today, approaches proliferate, and family therapy training institutes cross-pollinate them in major cities across the country. There is little focus on the emotional being of the therapist. Indeed, Bowen theory might say that the pursuit of data and technique through books and conferences resembles a form of substance abuse, binding the anxiety that will never really be reduced until the field focuses more on its own differentiation.

There is, however, a second, more important way in which Bowen theory would see family therapy as fused into society's anxiety: the tendency towards dichotomy rather than continuity in its thinking processes. This is a more fundamental issue because it is related to the structure of Bowen theory itself and its grounding in natural systems, and it illustrates how the theory could affect the emotional system of society on the deepest level — for, as mentioned, discontinuous classification is not confined to therapy but is found throughout the social sciences. Thus, from the perspective of Bowen theory, family therapy's fusion with society's anxiety does not begin "out in the field" when therapists start engaging with families, but is transmitted during our professional training and coded in the very methods of conceptualization employed by our institutions of learning. Or, to put it another way, the problem of reducing societal anxiety may lie less in changing "the family's construction of reality" (Reiss, 1981) than in reframing the therapist's (or therapy's) construction of reality — chiefly, the tendency in the social sciences to frame issues in terms of dichotomous, discontinuous either/or categories that often become the basis of polarization, rather than in terms of continuous, natural systems, emotional processes that link all symptoms, all people, and all generations. (And, since the structures of society are isomorphic to its anxiety, Bowen theory would link all academic disciplines, professional specialties, and their journals.)

The reason the conventional dichotomies in the social sciences reflect societal anxiety, according to Bowen theory, is that as thinking in any emotional system moves towards the either/or, all-or-nothing, black-or-white dichotomization of life, it begins to take on the characteristics of rigidity, concreteness, and lack of imagination that are found to be so blatant in the most anxiety-impaired members of our species. As mentioned above, there is a curious connection between the tendency to think in terms of either/or, all-or-nothing categories and the lack of resiliency of response in relationships. What schizophrenics are totally incapable of doing is thinking in terms of continua. And when societal anxiety becomes elevated, fundamentalism — that is, seeking certainty through reductionistic answers — increases.

This emphasis on the continuity of all emotional processes may be Bowen theory's most characteristic feature. It is what ultimately differentiates it from almost all other thinking in the social sciences. It is also what gives the theory the power to reframe the way questions have been traditionally posed. Bowen theory, therefore, is not simply a new set of answers, but is perhaps best understood as a new paradigm, that is, a new way of seeing. It pursues a different level of inquiry. It surrenders the promise of certainty on elementary cause-and-effect levels in order to obtain a broader (more objective) perspective. While an approach to change that questions the relevance of relevance may not stimulate avid political involvement, Bowen theory does contain the seeds of an upheaval potentially far more radical than the most status quo-disturbing social action. It is a revolution in what information is considered relevant to the process of change, and in the way problems are to be conceptualized.

I have tried to foreshadow this vital aspect of Bowen theory by highlighting throughout this essay some of the ways in which the theory makes continuous what other ways of thinking tend to dichotomize. It was shown, for example, that with regard to the human brain, Bowen saw degrees of reactivity as far more influential in human relationships or self-expression than right or left "brainedness." It was shown that a way of thinking about leadership that is far less given to polarization arises when leader and follower are seen as parts of an organic unit rather than as separate categories of a hierarchy. Similarly, it was shown how Bowen's focus on the nuclear family unit as the unit for treatment or observation blurred the distinctions among child problems, marriage problems, and individual health problems. With regard to therapy itself, it was shown how Bowen theory's emphasis on the differentiation of the therapist (his or her emotional being) diminished the significance normally accorded to different therapeutic techniques or distinctions between therapy and supervision. Similarly, it was shown how the focus on objectivity made the clinician and the researcher one.

To show the power for different conceptualizations that flows from Bowen's nondichotomous approach I will begin with four of the most influential, automatically accepted dichotomies in the social sciences — nature/nurture, body/mind, this culture/that culture, and male/female — and describe how Bowen theory would reformat all of these divisions in terms of continuous natural systems processes with the result that new questions arise about the structure and strategies of the helping professions. Then I will list many of the major dichotomies and polarizations characteristic of social science thinking and, next to each, also show the alternative, continuous level of inquiry that Bowen theory would focus on instead.

Some Generally Accepted Dichotomies

Nature/Nurture

The assumption that nature (genes) and nurture (environment) are separate, discontinuous elements in the development of humans fractionates thinking on many issues in both the mental and physical health fields. In some ways, this dichotomy almost organizes the helping establishment.

Bowen's notions of multigenerational transmission in an emotional field and of the nuclear family as an emotional unit suggest the possibility that emphasis on birth as a dividing line skews the reciprocal influences of this conventionally dichotomized pair. From the perspective of Bowen theory, family emotional factors could influence a child both mentally and physically, either before or after the child emerges from the womb. Such conceptualization even reframes the untouchable issue of acquired characteristics.

Body/Mind

While more and more attention has been given to psychosomatic medicine, both directly as well as through biofeedback and guided imagery, as the term "psychosomatic" conveys, most in the field still see the mind and the body as two discrete entities that affect one another rather than as elements that function as parts of each other within a broader field. Bowen's concept of differentiation and family emotional system rooted in natural evolutionary processes would conceptualize both body and mind as part of self, and relate all disease to problems of differentiation — what Kerr has referred to as "uni-disease." Focus on nuclear family emotional processes rather than on specific clinical entities unifies both ends of the body/mind dichotomy by establishing a different level of inquiry: an individual's position in his or her family emotional field. The body/mind dichotomy influences profoundly the way the helping professions are currently structured (it is the starting point for the division into specialties), and it establishes the criteria for the choice of a healer. Bowen theory would force us to ask to what extent the professional specialties that have evolved in our society reflect the range of dysfunction human organisms experience, and to what extent we think about ourselves the way we do because of the Yellow Page listings. More fundamentally, the continuous connection between mind and body that position in one's family emotional field establishes raises an even more disturbing question. If it is true that a very specific category of people become burdened with most of civilization's ills (if they do not get one thing, they will get another), how much progress will we really have made when we have cured cancer if we do not at the same time make progress in affecting multigenerational transmission? After all, homologously it may be the same thing.

This Culture/That Culture

As mentioned earlier, Bowen theory's focus on emotional process as a natural systems phenomenon rooted in and common to all protoplasm turns culture into the medium of expression rather than the driving force of family pathology. It suggests that when families hold their cultural background responsible for the way they function, not only is that not important information to jot down, but it is at that very moment *denial*, denial of personal responsibility (and avoidance of efforts at differentiation), as well as denial of the multigenerational transmission unique to that family. Focus on emotional processes rather than on culture also suggests that the differentiation of the therapist is far more critical in clinical outcomes than is his or her understanding of the client's background.

Male/Female

From the point of view of Bowen theory, all of the above would also hold true for the dichotomy of male/female. While this dichotomy is based on an obvious natural distinction and has been sharpened by the political concerns of the women's movement, when it comes to understanding families, or for that matter the "human phenomenon," Bowen theory would say that maturity (that is, differentiation or reactivity) is more significant than gender. Bowen theory would not deny the distinction between male and female or the sociological differences that have developed around it, but the theory would question whether information based on the gender dichotomy is the most significant information on which to base the process of changing emotional systems. It would say, rather, that nothing stated in this essay about triangles, differentiation, multigenerational transmission, or a person's position in his or her family emotional system is more accurate about one gender than about another — and that any given female person's vulnerability to dysfunction or capacity for recuperation can be predicted and promoted far better from information obtained from the bipolar graph than from data, accurate as such data may be, about physical or sociological differences between the sexes. This way of thinking also suggests that when choosing a healer, the differentiation of the professional (his or her capacity for self-regulation, nonreactivity, etc.) is a better criterion than his or her gender.

Conventional Dichotomy	Bowen Formulation
nature/nurture	multigenerational emotional processes
body/mind	family emotional field
this symptom/that symptom	nuclear family's level of chronic anxiety
one culture/another culture	family's own emotional process
male/female	maturity of response
right brain/left brain	reactivity
thinking/feeling	degree of self-differentiation
leader/follower	organizational emotional field
present/past	multigenerational transmission
supervision/therapy	self-regulation
research/practice	pursuit of objectivity
psychiatrist/psychologist (discipline)	capacity-to-think systems
this technique/that technique	differentiation of the healer
support/challenge	anxiety of the professional
insight/behavior	promoting differentiation
quit/adapt	sustain a nonreactive presence
independence/dependence	resiliency of the bond
toxic/nontoxic condition	response of the organism
cause/effect	change in the balance of the field
one age/another age	relational triangles
happy marriage/divorce	degree of nuclear family dysfunction
family system/work system	emotional process
a work system/a different industry	differentiation of the leader
one decision (choice)/another decision	maximizing objectivity

Bowen Theory and Social Science

In order to bring out more clearly the differences between Bowen theory and conventional social science formulations, particularly its overall characteristic of emphasis on continuity, I list some of the more common dichotomies found in the social sciences or family therapy, listed side by side with how Bowen theory would reframe that issue (see the chart above). Many have been mentioned separately in various parts of this essay; collectively, however, they show how far-reaching the continuity principle can be. In each case, the dichotomy listed on the left represents either a division basic to the thinking processes in the social sciences or a polarization around which choices are often made in therapy. The

Bowen formulation, listed on the right, in each case creates a different level of inquiry that turns the poles of the corresponding dichotomy into nodes within a continuous, natural systems process.

When a family is chronically polarized around specific issues, we know that the polarization is really an emotional phenomenon and is not due to the content of the dichotomy. Could the same be said about polarizations in the social sciences? Could the dichotomies listed above be emotional barriers that hinder our horizons and imaginative capacity, much as the equator did geographically for centuries? To continue the analogy, are the social sciences so bound up with certain unquestioned ways of organizing our minds that other information can never even be conceived of, no less recognized, until we can get past these barriers? Might the source of this way of conceptualizing be societal regression? Is it an anxious flight from responsibility that tends to support those forms of thinking that focus us on pathology (which has infinite capacity to spawn data) rather than on strength, which would then force us to focus on self, that is, differentiation? Is this the schizophrenia that Bowen says is in all of us? And, if that is so, as is often the case with severely impaired families, is our tendency towards dichotomous thinking the result of an emotional cutoff from previous generations? Bowen theory might suggest that the cutoff here is the primary discontinuity. It is the emotional cutoff that the social sciences have made with our natural systems link to our protoplasmic past, and it has had the same effect that cutoffs have in any family: we emphasize how we are different rather than how we are the same. Ultimately, from the point of view of Bowen theory, dichotomous formulations in the social sciences are not only discontinuous in their conception, but the very act of conceiving human problems in that mode discontinues us.

The journey of human thought constantly comes to crossroads, and the path chosen by the person leading the safari at that moment not only will describe (a view of) reality, but will also shape the reality of future generations by influencing what people see.

An interesting retrospective is provided by a long-lost paper by Freud published for the first time in English in 1987. In 1915, Freud wrote a paper entitled *A Phylogenetic Fantasy,* in which he suggested that modern anxiety is a form of reactivity transmitted by protoplasm from generation to generation since the trauma of the Ice Age. When the paper was rediscovered seventy years later, the psychoanalytic establishment went out of its way to show that it was wildly speculative. The major ideas — which come perilously close to Bowen's natural systems orientation, his theoretical grounding in evolutionary theory, and his notion of an emotional system — were not, they said, a part of the mainstream of Freud's thought. But they might have been. He wrote the paper during a period of great upheaval in traditional concepts of reality. The year 1915 was a decade past the year when Einstein published his special theory of relativity and the year before he published his general theory of relativity. It was also fifteen years after Max Planck put forth his quantum theory, which revolutionized conventional concepts of cause and effect, and for which he received a Nobel prize in 1918, three years after Freud wrote this monograph. For whatever reason, Freud continued down a mechanistic path of cause and effect. Had he continued to think out the ramifications of his Ice Age fantasy for the intergenerational links of human anxiety, not only might psychotherapy as the twentieth century has known it have taken a far different turn, but so might much of literature, education, the administration of court systems, and the manner in which the news media frame issues. Bowen theory may have a similar capacity to affect all dimensions of society.

There are, of course, problems with Bowen theory. No effort to encompass all of life's processes will ever be totally consistent. There will always be exceptions. Another problem is the tautological relationship between chronic anxiety and differentiation: levels of differentiation in a family both determine and are determined by the levels of chronic anxiety. As mentioned earlier, it is difficult to come up with criteria to show how one can disagree with, or not buy, Bowen theory and still claim to be differentiated. Do you have to think like Murray Bowen in order to understand his theory? The biggest problem with the theory is that it cannot be disproved. Basic to the acceptance of any theory for discussion is that it must set up the grounds for its own refutation (cf. solipsism or revelation). What kind of research project could prove it wrong? At the very least that fact lends credence to the previously stated view that Bowen theory and its therapeutic ramifications cannot be understood or evaluated through criteria drawn from another paradigm. It is, for better or for worse, its own paradigm.

Perhaps the best way to capture the complexities of Bowen theory's depth is to point out what many of us who have spent more than two decades trying to grasp its range and thrust repeat every few years, "I think I'm really beginning to understand it."

References and Bibliography

Beal, E., & G. Hochman (1991). *Adult children of divorce.* New York: Delacorte Press.

Bowen, M. (1978). *Family therapy in clinical practice.* New York: Jason Aronson.

Calhoun, J. B. (1963). *The ecology and sociology of the norway rat.* U.S. Department of Health, Education and Welfare/Public Health Service Publication Number 1008. Washington, DC: U.S. Government Printing Office.

Freud, S. (1987). *A phylogenetic fantasy* (translated by A. Hoffer & P. Hoffer). Cambridge, MA: Harvard University Press.

Friedman, E. (1982). *The myth of the shiksa.* In M. McGoldrick & B. Carter, eds. *Ethnicity and family therapy.* New York: Guilford Press.

Friedman, E. (1985). *Generation to generation: Family process in church and synagogue.* New York: Guilford Press.

Guerin, P. J., L. Fay, S. L. Burden, & J. C. Kauggo, J. C. (1967). *The evaluation and treatment of marital conflict.* New York: Basic Books.

Kerr, M. (1981). Family systems theory and therapy. In A. S. Gurman & D. P. Kniskern, eds., *Handbook of family therapy.* New York: Brunner/Mazel.

Kerr, M., & M. Bowen. (1988). *Family evaluation.* New York: Norton.

McGoldrick, M. & R. Gerson. (1985). *Genogram in family assessment.* New York: Norton.

McLean, P. (1985). Brain evolution related to family, play and the isolation call. *Archives of General Psychiatry.* 42:405–417.

Papero, D. (1990). *Bowen family system theory.* Needham Heights, MA: Allyn & Bacon, division of Simon & Schuster.

Pert, C. B. (1986). Wisdom of the receptors: Neuropeptides, the emotions, and bodymind. *Advances.* Institute for the Advancement of Health. 3:3.

Reiss, D. (1981). *The family's construction of reality.* Cambridge, MA: Harvard University Press.

Rasenbaum, L. (1989). *Biofeedback frontiers.* New York: AMS Press.

Sachs, L. (1986, January). Growth, differentiation, and the reversal of malignancy. *Scientific American.*

Sheldrake, R. (1988). *The presence of the past.* New York: Times Books.

Skinner, B. F. (1971). *Beyond freedom and dignity.* New York: A. A. Knopf.

Theodore, J. (1970, August 15). Distinction between "self" and "not-self" in lower invertebrates. *Nature.* 227.

Thomas, L. (1974). *Lives of a cell.* New York: Viking Press.

Titelman, P. (1987). *The therapist's own family: Toward the differentiation of self.* Northvale, NJ: Jason Aronson.

Toman, W. (1961). *Family constellation.* New York: Springer.

Webster, G., & B. C. Goodwin. (1982). The origin of species: A structural approach. *Journal of Biological Structure.* 5:15–47.

Zuckerman, H. (1967, November). The sociology of Nobel prize winners. *Scientific American.*

About Edwin H. Friedman

Born and raised in New York City, Edwin H. Friedman (1932–1996) was an ordained rabbi and practicing family therapist. Reared on Manhattan's Upper West Side, he graduated from Bucknell University and earned a doctorate of divinity at Hebrew Union College, where he was ordained in 1959.

Rabbi Friedman was intimately involved in politics, religion, and psychotherapy in the Washington, D.C., metropolitan area for nearly forty years. He was rabbi at Temple Shalom in Chevy Chase, Maryland, when he joined the Johnson White House as a community-relations specialist, and in 1964 he became the founding rabbi of the Bethesda Jewish Congregation.

His groundbreaking *Generation to Generation*, published in 1985, applies Bowen family systems theory to religious and other institutions. Praised by leaders of all faiths, it has become a handbook for understanding the connection between emotional process at home and at work in religious, educational, therapeutic, and business systems. It is now required reading in many universities and seminaries throughout the United States. *Friedman's Fables*, published in 1990, uses the ancient art form of the fable to offer fresh perspectives on human foibles, based on the author's insights into emotional process. Theories developed in his previous work have been extended to the concepts of leadership in *A Failure of Nerve: Leadership in the Age of the Quick Fix*, published after his death.

Friedman was in great demand as a consultant and public speaker, presenting workshops and lectures in almost every state and many countries before a wide variety of professional and lay audiences. During the last ten years of his life he led workshops for groups of Episcopal bishops, Trappist abbots and abbesses, members of Congress, state governors and their staffs, the General Staff of the United States Army in Europe, and the executive committee of the Chief of Naval Operations. His Center for Family Process in Bethesda trained people from the medical and psychotherapy professions as well as government and business leaders.

CPSIA information can be obtained
at www.ICGtesting.com
Printed in the USA
LVHW090434180719
624455LV00002B/86/P